Interface

Planetary Nodes

By

Michael Erlewine

Interface: Planetary Nodes

An ebook from

Startypes.com
315 Marion Avenue
Big Rapids, Michigan 49307

First published 1976

©2007 Michael Erlewine

ISBN 978-0-9798328-5-7

This book is dedicated to

Theodor Landscheidt
and
David W. Wilson

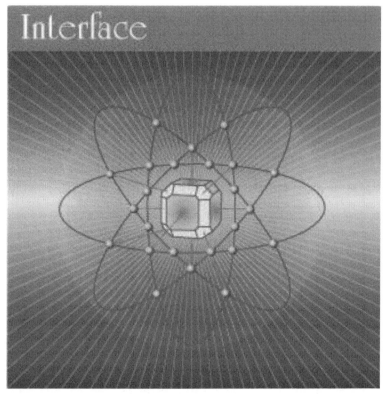

Interface: Planetary Nodes

Astrology is all about nodes. Nodes are sensitive points in the natal chart that can be interpreted. Obvious examples of nodes are the Nodes of the Moon. The Ascendant, Midheaven, Vertex and other sensitive horoscope points are nodes. The traditional twelve House Cusps are also nodes. Since most astrologers do not consider latitude when calculating aspects, even aspects are nodes.

We may be familiar with the above nodes, but what about planetary nodes? What are they?

What is a Node?

I had been studying astrology for some number of years before I understood what a node was, for example the Ascendant or Rising Sign that all astrologers mean when they ask: "What is your rising sign?"

Back then, my rising sign in Sagittarius, was to me just that: a point in the zodiac, in my case in the sign Sagittarius. It was not until much later that I understood that all nodes are intersections of two independent systems of one kind or another. In the case of my Ascendant, the zodiac was one system, but I had to research to find out the other, which turned out to be the Local Horizon.

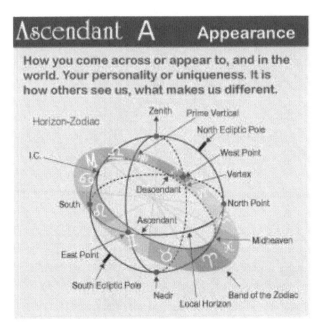

Ascendant A — Appearance

How you come across or appear to, and in the world. Your personality or uniqueness. It is how others see us, what makes us different.

The Ascendant is a Node

So the Ascendant is the intersection or interface between the plane of the zodiac and the plane of the local horizon, to the East. This was news to me and sent me scurrying to figure out what the other nodes I had always been using interfaced with.

For example, the Nodes of the Moon are the intersection of the plane of the Moon's orbit with the plane of Earth's orbit, the zodiac.

Or the Vertex is the intersection of the plane of the zodiac with the plane of what is called the Prime Vertical, a Great Circle running from East to West through the local Zenith. And so it went. You get the idea.

Interface: Planetary Nodes

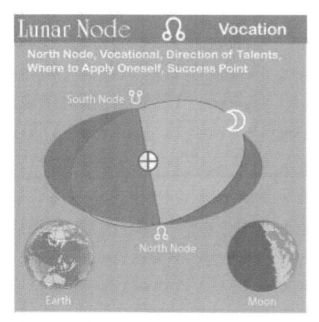

Lunar Node ♋ Vocation

North Node, Vocational, Direction of Talents, Where to Apply Oneself, Success Point

South Node ☋

North Node ☊

Earth

Moon

Nodes or Interfaces

The point here is that any node is an interface and intersection between two great circles or planes, very often involving the familiar zodiac. This book is about planetary nodes, the nodes or interfaces that are formed when the planes of any two planets intersect. And by intersect, I don't just mean intersect with the planet of the earth's orbit, but the planes of any two planets intersect with each other, with or without Earth being one of the two.

Two planetary planes intersect to create what we could call a sensitive point, more like a power point for that matter. As the planets travel around their orbits through time, they reach these power points or nodes two times in a complete orbit or cycle. At that point, the planet is not only in the plane of its own orbit, but simultaneously in the plane of the second planet, and this is a point of power or emphasis. This book is about the system of planetary nodes and how to interpret them in your own natal chart. I call these planetary nodes: "Interface Points."

Where it Started for Me

The interface concept came out of my interest in heliocentrics, in particular an inquiry into the mutual inclination (or lack thereof) of the various planes of our solar system, planes like that of the ecliptic, equator, horizon, galaxy, supergalaxy, and so on. I was fascinated by the different attitudes or inclinations of the various astronomical planes, each to the others. What could these mean?

Interface: Planetary Nodes

A whole series of astronomical coordinate systems exist, each with their own center and plane of reference. More interesting to me is that fact that these many systems are oriented to each other, differently — are set in space at different angles to one another. They are set in space like some grand crystal. Perhaps they represent whole approaches to life, each with its own independent attitude or stance.

I was interested to note that astrologers devote their attention to the zodiac or ecliptic, but seem to pay little or no attention to these other planes: the Horizon, Prime Vertical, and Celestial Equator. Astrologers seem not to grasp or care that points such as the Ascendant, MC, Vertex, etc. are not zodiac points alone, but are nodes representing the intersection of the zodiac with some other great plane. In fact, it takes two independent planes to create a node. This important fact seems to have been lost in modern astrology.

Even within our own solar system, each of the great planetary orbits has its own plane and particular orientation or attitude. Each of these great planetary orbital planes are oriented or inclined to the others. An attempt to reduce all these intersecting orbital planes -- this grand planetary crystal -- to the set of the most significant points or nodes was how the interface nodal technique came into being.

Interface: Planetary Nodes

Introduction to the Concept

As mentioned, astrologers use a variety of coordinate systems to look at life. The most well known, of course, is the zodiac or ecliptic system, but there are also the equatorial system of right ascension & declination, the horizon system of azimuth & altitude, the prime vertical system of longitude & amplitude, and still others.

On a grander scale, there are still other coordinate systems that are fascinating in their own right , including the local system of stars of which our Sun is a member, our own galactic system, and even a supergalactic system, of which I have written elsewhere ("The Astrology of Space." All in all, we have several major coordinate systems in common use by astrologers such as the ecliptic plus half a dozen or so esoteric systems that are little used, which brings me to concept of interface analysis.

Interface: Planetary Nodes

Interface analysis is a reduction of all of the nine planet's orbital planes, their inclinations and disinclinations to one another, to the particular series of zodiac points that represent both symbolically and physically the only points in the zodiac at which these various inclinations and disinclinations intersect and are exact or in perfect alignment.

When a planet (moving in its own orbit) comes into alignment with the orbital plane of a second planet (passes through or over that point), it is at one of the two nodes (ascending or descending) with that plane. I call these nodes 'Interface Points'. Therefore, an inclination or nodal alignment (interface) refers to an exact planar alignment between two planet's orbits (where the two planes intersect to form a node) and this will emphasize (for better or for worse) the nature and function of the planets involved. On the other hand, planets at DIS-inclination (at 90-degree points in their orbit to the nodes or interface points) represent these same principles as they are when most mutually disinclined — each to the other. It may help to offer a brief summary of the astronomical basis for this concept.

Interface: Planetary Nodes

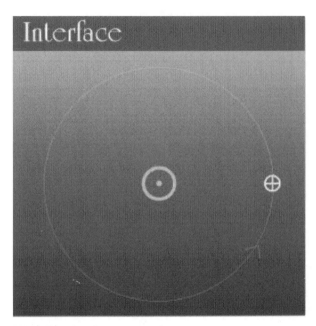

The Basic Astronomy

In the above diagram we see the Sun at the center of the solar system and Earth going counterclockwise (Looking down from above the Sun) in its almost circular orbit each year. The earth always stays in its orbit and that orbit defines a plane running through the center of the Sun and Earth. That plane geometrically extends infinitely in all directions, dividing the heavens into two halves, one above the orbit of the earth (and Sun) and the other below that orbit. This is standard high-school astronomy.

Interface: Planetary Nodes

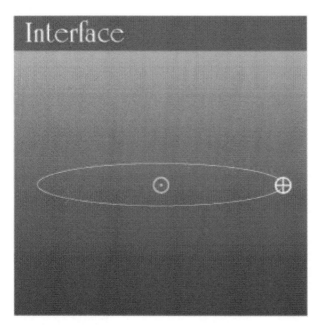

Earth's Orbital Plane

Here is the same diagram, but looking more or less from the side now, but at just enough of an angle so that you can see the ellipse of Earth's orbit. The earth's orbit, which defines the familiar zodiac or ecliptic, is the primary reference plane used by astrologers.

Interface: Planetary Nodes

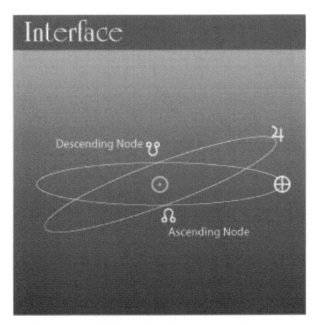

Nodes to Earth's Orbit

What is a node? As we know, each of the nine planets orbits around the Sun in a large ellipse, with the Sun as the center. This orbital ellipse of the earth and any planets defines a plane passing through the center of the Sun. The planes of the orbits of the nine planets in our solar system do not happen to coincide (do not orbit in the same plane), but, instead, are inclined to one another, slightly. The line defined by the intersection of the planes of any two planetary orbits is called the line of nodes.

In the above diagram we can see the orbit of the earth and the orbital plane of the planet Jupiter. Note that these two orbital planes cross each other to form two intersections or interfaces. These are the planetary nodes of Jupiter and Earth. Both the ascending and descending nodes are marked in the diagram.

Interface: Planetary Nodes

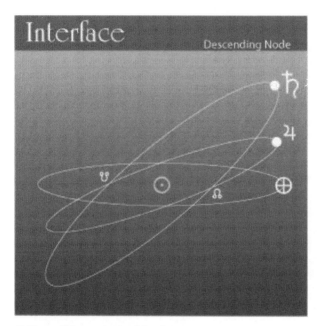

Other Planetary Nodes

Our solar system has the Sun at its center and this is known as the heliocentric celestial sphere. Since all of the planetary orbital planes pass (by definition) through the center of the Sun, the planes all intersect the celestial sphere in what are called great circles. Therefore, each intersecting planetary plane has a distinct pair of nodes with each of the other planets, thus the system of planetary nodes.

This pair of nodes for each planetary pair (Mercury-Venus, Mars-Saturn, etc.) represents the two points in the zodiac (ascending and descending nodes) where *either* planet is simultaneously in both planes at once.

23

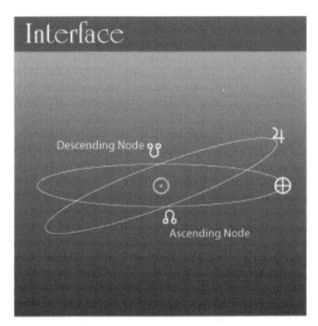

Nodes to Earth

For example, the planetary nodes of all the other planets with respect to the Earth (i.e. where their planes intersect the Earth's orbital plane — the ecliptic) and the inclinations of these planes to the Earth's orbital plane are known to astrologers, although even these points are not often used in modern astrology.

There is, however, some small reference in the astrological literature to a planet being at its node in the plane of the Earth. For instance: Jupiter might be sighted as being at its northern or southern node to the Earth plane, and yet seldom (almost never) do we find reference to the Earth being at this same nodal point (and in the Jupiterian plane), although this happens without fail twice a year! At these times, the Earth moves into alignment with the Jupiter plane and takes on some of the qualities of that planet.

Interface: Planetary Nodes

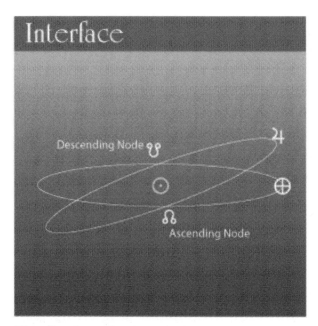

Interface

Descending Node ☍

♃

☉

⊕

☋

Ascending Node

The Jupiter-Earth Interface

In the above diagram, you can see where the plane of Jupiter's orbit intersects with the plane of Earth's orbit.

My point is that: while astrologers have embraced and often use the concept of planetary pairs when it comes to aspects, we have managed to ignore these nodal pairs, although they are *at least* as physically valid as aspects. As we know, astrologers have a plethora of riches when it comes to the myriad points and techniques available to them.

Until this writing (1976), almost no attention has been given to the fact that each pair of planetary orbits intersect one another to produce their particular set of nodal intersections, irrespective of the orbit of the Earth. It is this last category that is the particular subject of this book.

The Planetary Nodes Exclusive of Earth

The Earth is but one planet, albeit a very important one to us, in our solar system. What we are examining here (which are not so familiar, although easily computed) are the nodes (points in the zodiac) where any two planets' orbital planes (irrespective of the Earth's plane) intersect. This article is concerned with the location of the entire system of planetary-pair nodal points (interface points) as they can be measured along the zodiac.

Interface: Planetary Nodes

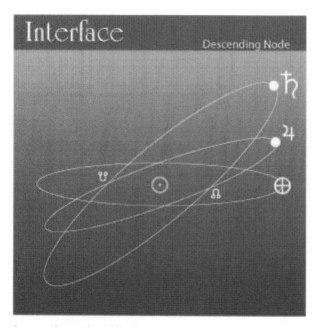

Locating the Nodes

Let's consider any two planets other than the Earth, for example: Jupiter and Saturn. The planes of their orbits make great circles on the Celestial Sphere as does the plane of Earth's orbit. Where these two great planes intersect one another are the planetary nodes or interface points for this particular planetary pair. Now let's zoom in on where these three planes (Earth, Jupiter, and Saturn) interface.

27

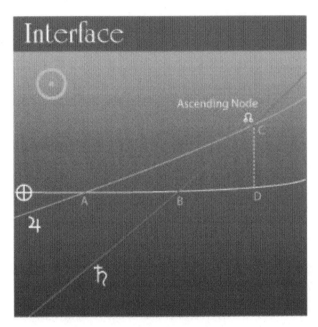

Close Up of n Interface Point

Note that these points are located slightly above or below the zodiac plane (Earth plane), but not right in it. Since most astrologers have only the zodiac as their plane of reference, it is convenient to use this zodiac in order to point out activities in these other planes. With the help of mathematician David W. Wilson and using spherical trigonometry, we have projected these points on to the astrological zodiac (ecliptic), so that by watching either Mars or Saturn transit a given point in our zodiac (using the heliocentric ephemeris), we can know that the planet (either Mars or Saturn) is simultaneously at its interface and exactly in the plane of the second planet. The result is an easy way for us to tell when a planet is at a particular interface point, by using a standard heliocentric ephemeris.

Interface: Planetary Nodes

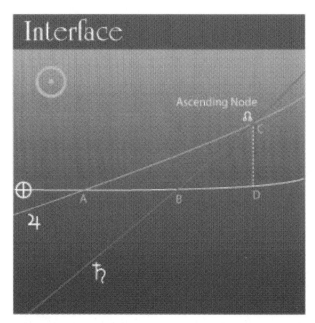

Ecliptic Intercepts

In the above diagram, we are looking at the ascending or northern node the Saturn plane to the Jupiter plane, the Saturn-Jupiter interface point. This is marked by point "C." The point where Saturn crosses Earth's plane (zodiac) is point "B," and the point where Jupiter crosses the zodiac is point "A." If we project point "C" down to the zodiac at point "D," then whenever either Jupiter or Saturn reach point "D" using any heliocentric ephemeris, we can know that the planet (Jupiter or Saturn) is then at is interface point to the Jupiter and Saturn plane.

In other words, the tables at the end of this article list the points in the zodiac when the particular planetary-pair node or interface is exact in the planes of the two planets involved. Now let's look at the system of interface points from a less technical viewpoint.

Nodal Points in Astrological Work

Let us briefly review the use of nodes in modern astrology:

As mentioned earlier, astrology is very nodal, more than one might at first imagine. This article concentrates on the planetary nodes. However, just in passing, you may wish to note that standard points like the Ascendant and Vertex are nothing more than nodes. And it always takes the planes of two independent coordinate systems to create a node.

While astrologers are aware that points like the Ascendant and Vertex are zodiac points, many are not aware that the Ascendant (for example) is brought to you by means of the zodiac AND another independent plane, that of the Local Horizon. The Ascendant is where they intersect, the intersection of the plane of the zodiac and the plane of the local horizon to form a line of nodes.

Interface: Planetary Nodes

Still fewer astrologers know that the Vertex is made available by the intersecting plane of the Prime Vertical coordinate system (again, to the plane of the zodiac). In fact, most of the hot spots of astrology are where two coordinates systems come together to intersect and create an interesting set of nodes or points. So much of our astrology concerns itself only with the familiar zodiac that there is little awareness of the many supporting systems of coordinates that are also in effect.

Astrology

Lunar Nodes

Representing the interrelationship of the orbital plane of the moon with that of the Earth, the lunar nodes are widely used and understood by practically all modern astrologers, both in the East and the West. There are several good texts available on these nodes and I refer you to those.

Interface: Planetary Nodes

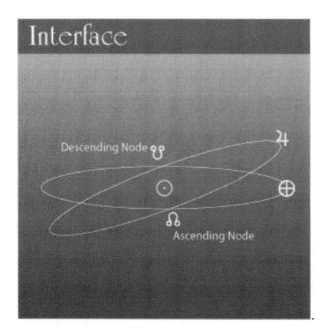

Planetary Nodes

The use of the planetary nodes in modern astrology is generally restricted to the nodes of the various planets as they intersect the orbital plane of the Earth (the zodiac or ecliptic). The planar interfacial angles of the other planets relative to each other (planetary nodes) have been practically ignored.

As an example of this ignorance, let me cite the continual reference in the astrological literature to a planet being at its node in the plane of the Earth. For instance: Jupiter, as pointed out earlier, is often cited as being at its northern or southern node — and yet seldom (almost never) do we find reference to the Earth being at this same nodal point (and in the Jupiter plane) although, as mentioned above, this happens two times a year. At these times, the Earth moves into the Jupiter plane and takes on some of the qualities of that planet.

Interface: Planetary Nodes

Interface

Interface: Mutual Intersection

In brief, the primary reason why the planetary nodes are not more widely used and appreciated by astrologers is the failure to realize these points in their reciprocity – equal-"ness." A planetary nodal point, by definition, represents the mutual intersection of two independent (planetary orbital) planes. We have chosen to call these nodal points 'Interface Points', as this word emphasizes the reciprocal nature of any single point and plane. A node points both ways.

Realization of these nodal lines as planetary pairs that represent the nature of both planets involved will result in more wide-spread use of these interface points and their incorporation into the body of technique as practiced by the astrologers of today.

Interface: Planetary Nodes

Interface Summary

In summary, the structure of our solar system is in fact defined by the interrelationship of the various orbital planes of which it is composed. This interrelationship is conveniently expressed by the complete system of planetary nodes and their square points. In this introduction to the use of these nodes by astrologers, we will confine ourselves to activation of these nodal points by direct transit at the Interface node shared by any two planets *and* activation by transit to points square (at ninety degrees) from these interface nodal points. Let's discuss the "Square Points."

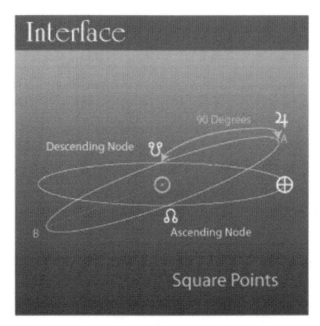

The 90-Degree or Square Points

In the above diagram, note points "A" and "B." This are the points in the orbit when the planet is 'square" or 90-degrees from either node. At these ninety degree or square points, a planet reaches what is astronomically termed its point of greatest latitude (either north or south) to the plane of the second planet involved. These points of greatest latitude are those points where the planet is most highly disinclined (literally) to the plane of the second planet and simultaneously changes reference from one node and begins to move (in its orbit) toward a conjunction with the opposite node.

In the above diagram, Jupiter is 90-degrees from either the ascending or descending node, and is as dis-inclined to Earth as it ever gets. Point "B" is the opposite point, beneath the earth's orbital plane.

Interface: Planetary Nodes

Changing-Lines

Therefore, you will note that at these Square Points we have a changing-line of relationship, while at the interface nodal points themselves, we have the simple activation or direct function of the principles involved.

To repeat: activation of the interface points themselves by transit of either of the two planets involved results in simple emphasis and clear function. For instance: one planet will be, by transit, in the plane of the second. The second planet (somewhere in its own orbit) is always in its own plane and yet, for a time (long or short, depending on the planets involved), the first planet is, by transit, exactly in this same plane and may be said to take on some of its qualities, whether by resonance or some other undetermined means.

It is important to have in mind which plane is being activated and which planet is, by transit, active in that plane. Is Mars by transit in the plane of Saturn or is Saturn transiting in the plane of Mars or both — which happens occasionally. These distinctions, at first perhaps somewhat confusing, will become clear with some study and you may be satisfied, to begin with, keeping simply in mind that the Saturn/Mars Interface is in activation.

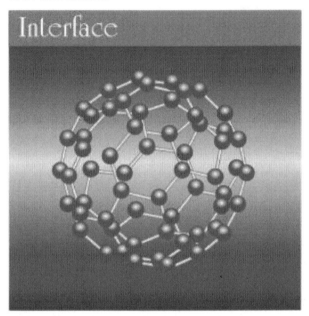

Questions of Interpretation

The simple and very defined structure and interrelationship of these various points tend to dictate concerning questions of interpretation, and one advantage to this approach is that very little is left to the imagination which, for some astrologers, can be a decided blessing. The relationships are clear:

The northern (or ascending) node of a planet is that point where the planet transits a given plane in what is called a south to north direction (from under to above the given plane). The southern or descending node is a transit from north to south (above to below the given plane). Above and below are defined by the position of the north pole of the ecliptic.

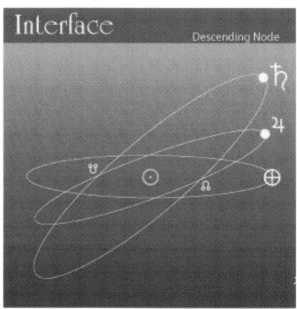

In Review

A given planet (such as Jupiter) transits a node to the plane of a second planet (say, Saturn), at which time Jupiter is perfectly in the plane of the second planet, Saturn. Jupiter then continues along its orbit (away from that node) until the point is reached of greatest latitude (whether north or south) in relation to the nodal interface in question. From that moment onward, the planet (Jupiter, again) proceeds to move toward the opposite nodal point for the particular planetary pair and once again (at the opposing node) comes directly into the plane of the planet to be transited, Saturn.

Therefore: matters of interpretation are somewhat simplified and restricted (at least at first) to an analysis of the various quadrants: transit to the nodes and to the points of greatest disinclination (above and below) to these nodes.

Activation of the meaning of the interface points themselves needs no lengthy introduction here since there are many fine texts available that spell-out every possible planetary combination. Students are referred to Reinhold. Ebertin's *"The Combination of Stellar Influences"* as one of the best of its kind, although sometimes a bit dark or too heavy. I have also written all of these combinations as well, and they are available in some of my books and software programs.

Interface: Planetary Nodes

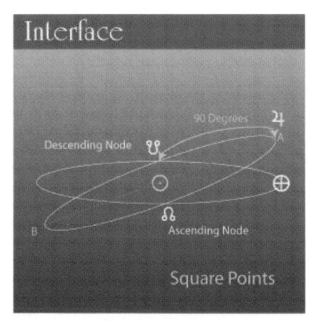

Changing-Lines or Square Points

Although the planetary combinations are well known from other forms of astrology, we will spend some time here in the presentation of the principles involved in an understanding as to the use of the Square or Changing-Line points. These changing-line points, when activated, represent simultaneously two ideas:

(1) A planet at these points is as out-of-plane and therefore as disinclined as it can ever be to the plane of the second planet.

(2) At the same time the planet is changing its relationship to the nodal axis itself — away from one node and toward the opposite node.

A close study of these changing points will reveal much as to changing (uneasy, <u>dis</u>-eased, disinclinations, etc.), while the interface points themselves offer the more straight-forward function of the planetary pairs (nodes) involved.

Consideration of all the planet's orbits simultaneously presents an ever-changing — almost kaleidoscopic effect — very similar to that obtained when rotating a fairly complex crystal in sunlight. Mutual harmonics and complex interrelationships are revealed that often highlight a single planet — again and again.

Therefore it is entirely possible, using only the interface points and their changing-lines or square points to reveal a structure indicative of the whole-life force of the individual or event being examined. In practice, however, best results are obtained when interface analysis is combined along with other traditional heliocentric or geocentric astrological techniques.

The Planes or Chakras

Although this is not meant primarily to be an section on the interpretation of the various planets and the planes they describe, some brief mention of the principles involved in such an interpretation is warranted. The planes or levels described by the planets are exactly similar to what in the Eastern tradition are termed chakras, the centers of force and activity which make up the whole of our life. A particular individual, while a part of this whole system, is usually more active and concerned with one level of their lives than with the others, at least at any given time.

Interface analysis has proved to be a great help in locating the specific level (chakra or plane) and planet to which an individual naturally responds. Once this is revealed, information is easily forthcoming of direct interest to the individual concerning the particular

plane of life and initiation in which they are finding
themselves involved.

Inner the Key to the Outer

For a more complete description of these various
planets or chakras — please see my book "*Astrology
of the Heart – Astro-Shamanism.*" The basic idea may
be expressed here in one sentence: the key to the
outer will always be the inner or in other words: the
key to a given planet (chakra) will usually be that
planet whose orbit is immediately within or inside the
planet in question.

A perfect and clear example: the planet immediately
within the Earth's orbit is Venus and for all time the
Earth has been ever concerned with Venus or love
and, in fact, divine love has always been put forth by
the world's spiritual lights as the very <u>key</u> to life on this
planet.

Interface: Planetary Nodes

Interface

Initiation in the Planes

This is equally true for all planets from and including Saturn into the Sun (The outer planets have a different significance). It should be understood that, although we live by virtue of our birth on this planet, we are not by that fact automatically in full realization of our Earth existence. In fact, initiation within inner planes (planets) is a gradual process of graduation, by degrees.

The majority of us have great difficulty working through (for instance) the Saturn (Satan), Jupiter (succession), and Mars (marriage) to even get in possession of the Earth (the Heart or child) much less graduating to the inner planes of Venus (divine love), Mercury (light of love), and on to the Sun (Self or 1000-petaled chakra).

Levels of Life

As remote and "flowery" (or vague or abstract) as the above sentences may seem to some readers, it is important to understand these various planes and to realize that we in fact find ourselves endlessly involved, evolving, and revolving through this life. At any one time a given individual will be taken up with concerns of a given plane or chakra. It becomes of great importance to the counseling astrologer to accurately indicate at what level and plane the life is being extended or occurring and to what plane the individual may be referred to for more light and a clear answer as to the questions they may have.

In practice, the role of the astrologer often involves directing and referring individuals to the level or chakra which happens to be the key to their current life's concern. Interface Node analysis can help astrologers to more accurately and without personal bias determine the levels or planes to which a given individual responds as well as the key or level to be recommended as a way to these inner planes.

Interface Analysis

In the past, astrologers have too often been limited and restricted in their practice to those chakras or planets in which they personally may have taken initiation (understand from personal experience) and they have primarily worked only with those clients who exist on an outer planet or plane of initiation from their own level -- less aware than they are.

It is possible using Interface analysis for the astrologer to accurately determine and to direct a client to the appropriate level or plane, regardless of whether he or she personally has (or has not) taken that particular initiation. To do this with accuracy demands a relatively absolute frame of reference to which all matters may be referred. The simple structure of our solar system is such a framework and when properly understood and rigorously applied, much of what amounts to guesswork in the practice of astrology is removed.

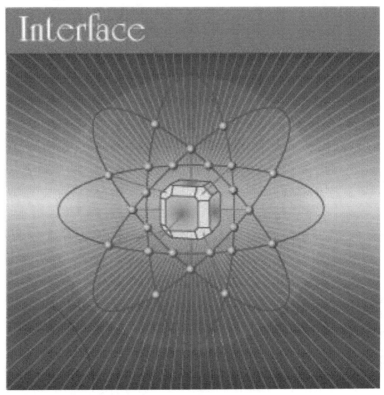

The Astrologer of this Aquarian Age

Since the primary use of astrology in my life has been to confirm my own inherent nature and to explain to myself what I find happening around me, I would like to mention briefly some benefits of this technique of a more personal and yet still absolutely useful nature. To cite a personal instance: in my natal heliocentric configurations, I have the planets

Interface: Planetary Nodes

Venus/Neptune/Jupiter mutually inclined to each other. In my younger (and not-so-younger) years, one source of concern and confusion for me involved periodic encounters with people with whom I didn't by nature get along. Some folks even took a dislike to me. Imagine that!

I always wondered why and I spent an unwarranted amount of energy and time searching myself to discover what I could have done to offend or to deserve such a reception. After all, we would all prefer to be loved and appreciated.

Exploring Interface Nodes

With this in mind, it was most satisfying, not to mention fascinating, to discover in the helio natal charts of these particular individuals who seemingly took offense to myself, that they had one or more planets at the changing-line or square point to my natal Jupiter/Venus or Neptune. In other words, they were most definitely disinclined to the planets to which I was by nature perfectly inclined.

Seeing this spelled out to me in their natal configurations has helped me to realize the simple fact of these inclinations/disinclinations, and to let pass the endless opportunities to search and question myself as to the fault -- on either part -- for this fact.

Interface: Planetary Nodes

On the other hand, I was interested to discover that in almost every instance, my closest personal friends all had the same planets at the same degree and that this degree was an Interface point that was perfectly complementary (inclined) to myself -- my inclinations. This was (in my life) a rather remarkable discovery and one with the most practical kind of benefits to me as to the time and energy previously wasted in a useless self-examination. This is an example of how astrology has benefited me. Enough said.

A System of Notation

It remains for us to discuss a convenient system of notation by which to represent these Interface points, as they are found in a given chart. Such a system must include the planets themselves in their order from the Sun outward. A vertical column (like the spinal column) is perhaps symbolically the most correct.

Taking a particular natal or event chart (heliocentric only), we examine each planet's position and compare these positions to the list of interface points. We will want to notate activity at both the Interface points and the square or changing-line points.

Interface: Planetary Nodes

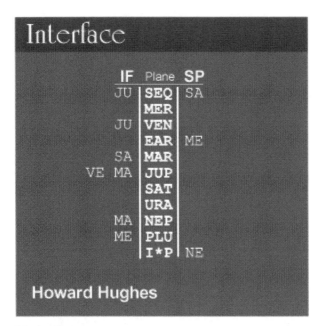

	IF	Plane	SP	
	JU	SEQ	SA	
		MER		
	JU	VEN		
		EAR	ME	
	SA	MAR		
VE	MA	JUP		
		SAT		
		URA		
	MA	NEP		
	ME	PLU		
		I*P	NE	

Howard Hughes

Notation

The yellow column in the center represents the planetary planes, much like the chakra centers said to be along the human spine. It is useful to think of this column in that way.

To the left of that column are the moving or transiting planets, planets that are at the Interface Point with another planet. If a planet is listed on the left, it means it is at the interface point and thus 'in the plane' of the planet listed in the central column. It is 'inclined' and in the plane of the other planet, the one listed in the central column

If a planet is listed to the right of the central column, it means this planet is at the Square Point (Changing line) and is 'disinclined' or at the 90-degree pointed between the two nodes and as 'not in the plane' as physically possible.

53

Interface: Planetary Nodes

Using this system of notation, you can see at a glance even complex arrangements of Interface and Square Points. Whole little trees can be read at a glance.

Interface: Planetary Nodes

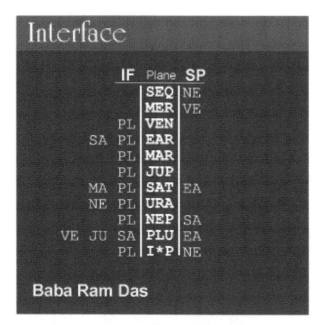

Interface Tree for Baba Ram Das

I have included below the "trees" of several well known individuals. You will note that the tree for Baba Ram Das, who personally withstood public opinion concerning the greatly feared psychedelic drug LSD, has the Interface Jupiter-Pluto simultaneously activated by both Pluto and Jupiter. These planets are also in conjunction in this natal chart (helio).

Jupiter (Sanskrit: Guru) represents the Life Path or literally the "way to go," and Pluto represents transformation, so these mutually reciprocal planets are clear and easy to interpret.

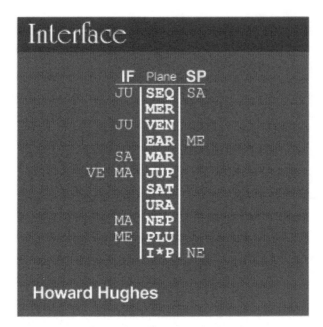

Interface

IF	Plane	SP
JU	SEQ	SA
	MER	
JU	VEN	
	EAR	ME
SA	MAR	
VE MA	JUP	
	SAT	
	URA	
MA	NEP	
ME	PLU	
	I*P	NE

Howard Hughes

Interface Tree for Howard Hughes

The tree for Howard Hughes has another mutual activation, in this case between Jupiter and Venus. What could be a better indication of wealth than a Venus-Jupiter combination? In Hughe's case, he has both planets, each at the other's interface. Jupiter is at the interface (and thus in the plane) of Venus, and Venus is at the interface (and thus in the plane) of Jupiter.

Interface: Planetary Nodes

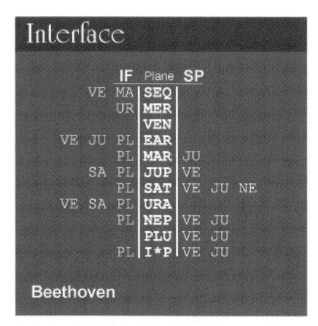

```
Interface

         IF   Plane   SP
      VE MA  | SEQ |
         UR  | MER |
             | VEN |
   VE JU PL  | EAR |
         PL  | MAR | JU
      SA PL  | JUP | VE
         PL  | SAT | VE JU NE
   VE SA PL  | URA |
         PL  | NEP | VE JU
             | PLU | VE JU
         PL  | I*P | VE JU

Beethoven
```

Interface Tree for Beethoven

And Beethoven's chart has an extraordinary emphasis on the planet Pluto, as does that of Baba Ram Das. You will also note that the planes or chakras most active in the Hughes chart are the middle-body chakras (Mars and Jupiter), while Baba Ram Das is more active in the outer planets. Beethoven sort of has the whole interface tree lit up. Points of disinclination show in Beethoven's chart some difficulty with the Mars principle (the marriage or emotions), while in the other diagrams Mercury and Earth are featured in DIS-inclination.

It remains for those of you who can respond to the ideas presented here to investigate for yourselves this fascinating subject and determine its usefulness in your particular work. In our understanding, what is revealed through this system of Interface points is exactly what is presented in the whole of chapter four of the Book of Revelations.

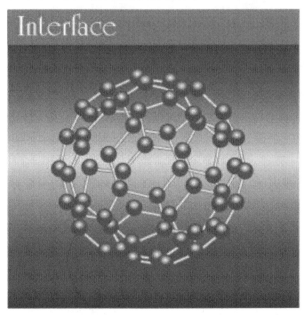

Not Geocentric

Note: Attempts to apply these points to the geocentric natal chart would be practical only with the outer planets, where the difference between geo and helio positions is plus or minus about three degrees and with the Earth/Sun axis, which is identical in either coordinate system. It is time that modern astrologers exercise their understanding of the fact, in addition to our lives on earth, we live simultaneously the lives of our solar system and Galaxy. We share a common fate. The heliocentric coordinate system may still be new to astrologers as a system of measurement, but the experience to which it refers is not new. It is where we came from and still are living.

Age of Aquarius

The religions of this world have long championed a more inclusive reality and each of us has for days or parts of days in our lives sustained awareness of this greater life. We have in fact arrived at a point where this experience can be measured and studied. As astrologers, we can point out to the world the opening in our times of what has been called the Age of Aquarius, a time of group work and mass understanding (initiation).

What more appropriate sign of this new age might we expect than a more holistic representation of this larger self to which we are true and an ability to refer and measure this self through coordinate systems of increasing inclusiveness. The net result is not a desertion of the geocentric (body) perspective, but rather the enhancement of that perspective, "To see eternity in a grain of sand."

Measuring Eternity

As astrologers we are concerned with realizing eternity as it exists captured in the geocentric circumstances inherent in individual existence. We do not forsake the geo for the helio, as some have suggested. We in fact live at once through all time and all space and: This is it! All coordinate systems demonstrate this principle and exist only as they are convenient modes in which to measure and realize Eternity.

Bibliography

Interface: Planetary Nodes by Michael & Margaret Erlewine and David W. Wilson, Heart Center Books, 1976.

Interface Analysis by Michael Erlewine, NCGR Journal, 1977.

Astrology of the Heart: Astro-shamanism, by Michael Erlewine, e-book, available online.

The Astrology of Space, by Michael Erlewine, e-book, available online.

Interface Interpretations

Before we get into some example interpretations of both the Interface Points and the Square Points, it is important to say something about the two planes with which you may not be familiar with, the plane of the Sun's Equator and the Invariable Plane of the solar system.

Interface: Planetary Nodes

Invariable Plane of the Solar System

The Invariable Plane of our solar system passes through the center of gravity of the solar system and is independent of the mutual perturbations of the planets. It is called 'invariable' because it remains unaltered, regardless of any and all motions within the planetary system. It is a plane through the center of mass, perpendicular to the orbital angular-momentum factor. This factor is made up of the angular momentum arising from orbital revolutions and from axial rotations.

As one planet decreases its eccentricity and inclination (over very long time periods), one or more orbits must at the same time be increasing their eccentricities and inclinations, whereby the total amount of eccentricity and inclination remains constant. Jupiter and Saturn largely determine the invariable plane, since they are the largest and

63

heaviest of the planets. There has been some thought given to using the invariable plane as a fundamental reference plane on which to study planetary configurations. The center of mass of the solar system moves, with respect to the inertial system of reference, in a straight line with constant speed through space in a 250-million-year orbit or circle around the galactic center. The northern node of the invariable plane to the ecliptic is 107°03'46.99" in longitude (1950.0) with an inclination of 1°34'50" to the ecliptic plane. Thanks to Charles A. Jayne, Jr. for his original research on this subject.

Interface: Planetary Nodes

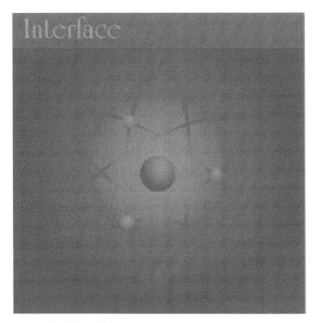

Invariable Plane: Interpretation

As for interpreting the Invariable Plane, as far as I know no one has ever done it, at least when this book was first published in 1976. Here is how I think of it:

If a planet is in synch and at the Interface Point with the Invariable Plane of the solar system, it is in some way in synch or harmony with the fundamental physical plane of the momentum of the entire solar system. In other, words it has a lot of stability backing it up. So I tend to interpret such an interface as very stable and solid, like a rock, and any planet in that plane has some added stability and can't be budged. I hope that helps, but check it out for yourself. All of this is still very new.

Interface: Planetary Nodes

Invariable Plane Specs

SS-105 North Pole of Invariable Plane
17°Ar03'41 +88°25'10

SS-106 South Pole of Invariable Plane
17°Le52'17 -87°48'04

SS-107 Ascending North Node Invariable Plane to
ecliptic = 17°Cn03'47 - 0°00'00

SS-108 Descending South Node Invariable Plane to
ecliptic = 17°Cp09'11 + 0°42'26

SS-109 Ascending North Node Invariable Plane to
equator =03°Ar32'48 - 1°32'13

SS-110 Descending South Node Invariable Plane to
equator =03°Li32'48 + 1°32'13

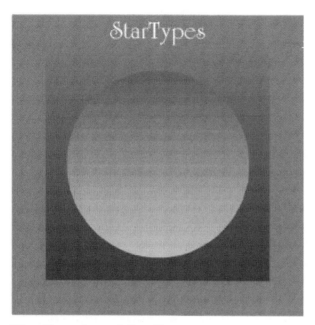

The Equator of the Sun

The equator of the Sun is another fundamental reference plane to which we could refer all planetary motion. The inclination of the solar equator to the ecliptic is 7°15' and the longitude of the ascending node to the ecliptic of 1950 is 75°04'. The plane of the Sun's equator is of course an important reference point in the solar system and where that plane intersects with the plane of the earth's orbit is something worth noting and considering. For that matter, the same goes for the intersection of the Solar Equator with the planes of all the other planets, not just Earth.

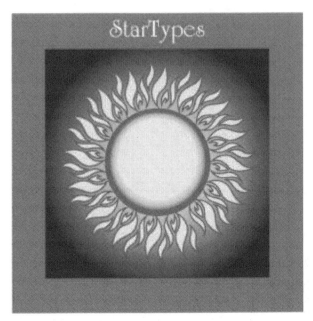

Similar to the Moon's Nodes

Most astrologers are aware of the lunar nodes, which represent the intersection of the plane of the lunar orbit with the plane of the earth's orbit. After all, these nodes are part of how we determine eclipses. The lunar nodes are interpreted and used by most astrologers.

The Solar Nodes should be interpreted just as we interpret the lunar nodes, but rather than refer to the Moon, the reference here is to the Sun. For example:

If the lunar nodes refer to where we can look for support and nurture, then the solar nodes point to where we can look for inspiration and to catch a glimpse of our potential future. The Solar Nodes are every bit as important as the lunar nodes, but have been overlooked by most astrologers.

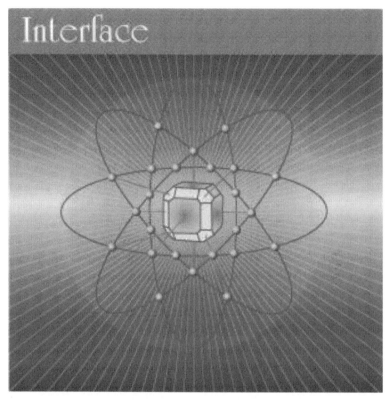

The Interpretations

What follows are general interpretations of each planet in each of both the Interface Point (and plane) and at the Square Points or disinclined to the plane and Interface Point. Please accept that this is but an opening statement on what is still a very new area of astrology. Most important will be to check out your own chart by looking at the tables at the end of this book.

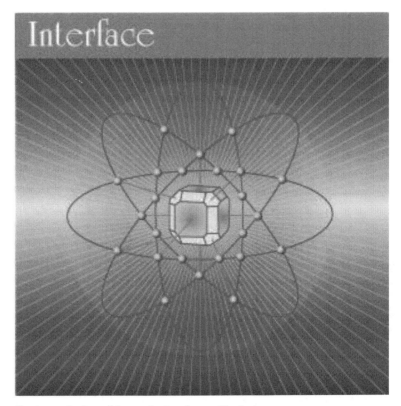

Determining Your Interface Points

In order to check out your Interface Nodes and Square Points, you will need a copy of your heliocentric chart. Virtually all astrological software offers at least a listing of your heliocentric planet positions. I have even seen free online services.

Once you have your helio chart, you have the zodiac position for each planet. Just look them up in the tables at the end of this book, and write down the various nodes and square points as shown elsewhere in this book. Then look up the interpretation for each node or square point.

Interface: Planetary Nodes

The Solar Equator

Mercury in the Plane of Sun's Equator

You whole sense of yourself is naturally mercurial, and thoughts, thinking them, and wit of all kinds are as natural for you as a sunny day. Your mind may be your most valuable asset.

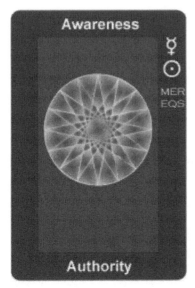

Mercury Square the Plane of Sun's Equator

You don't fancy yourself a great thinker, and pontificating with endless thoughts and ideas are just not how you see yourself. You choose a more practical and perhaps simple mental path.

Venus in the Plane of Sun's Equator

You love yourself, naturally, and everyone who knows you sees this. But you also have a deep reverence for just about any and all parts of life, and those around you can see this too. In fact, the way you care and show your appreciation for life amounts to a lesson for the rest of us on how to enjoy life.

Venus Square the Plane of Sun's Equator

Whatever you may like or dislike in life, you don't always end up liking yourself a whole bunch. This is something you should become aware of and compensate for. Learning to appreciate and enjoy yourself may be for you a somewhat bitter pill.

Interface: Planetary Nodes

Earth in the Plane of Sun's Equator

An almost magical sense of destiny and a larger-than-life sense of yourself, as if your tailor made to play a great part in whatever facet of life you are involved in.

Interface: Planetary Nodes

Earth Square the Plane of Sun's Equator

A struggle at times for self confidence, perhaps not being seen or heard in some sense. At odds with one's own self.

Mars in the Plane of Sun's Equator

You feel good about yourself, who you are, where you are going, and are not at all bashful about it. Your drive for the future and strong feelings of your self are something of a calling card with you. Everyone else is clear about this.

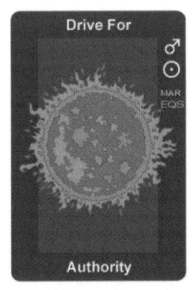

Mars Square the Plane of Sun's Equator

Your own feelings and drive may at times work against your own best interests, and create future obstacles that will have to be negotiated down the line. You don't always feel your self.

Jupiter in the Plane of Sun's Equator

You may well be attracted to a career that features you, rather than keep your self on the back burner. You naturally promote yourself in what you do and this may be a key part of your personality.

Jupiter Square the Plane of Sun's Equator

Your career may not be all that self-fulfilling, and more a means to an end rather than an end in itself. You may look elsewhere in your life for self-fulfillment.

Saturn in the Plane of Sun's Equator

Your hard-work ethic, adherence to rules and regulations, and no-nonsense approach is so natural to you that it is obviously just an essential part of yourself, just who you are.

Saturn Square the Plane of Sun's Equator

You like to bend the rules, get around regulations, and out-and-out confront the authorities from time to time. Discipline and hard work are not a good fit for your sense of yourself.

Interface: Planetary Nodes

Uranus in the Plane of Sun's Equator

You may draw attention to yourself through your non-conformity and more than a trace of a rebellious nature. That suits you just fine, like a fine glove. You are the paradigm of the inventor or discoverer, always searching new ground.

Uranus Square the Plane of Sun's Equator

Whatever non-conformist and rebellious traces you have never manage to bring you much forward motion or productivity. With you, the unconventional is more like working against your own self interests.

Neptune in the Plane of Sun's Equator

You are naturally quite the charmer and it oozes out of your self like sunlight from shadow. You have a natural ability to entrance and entertain, whisking your audience outside the bonds of everyday life and on to something more, perhaps through music, speaking, or theater.

Neptune Square the Plane of Sun's Equator

As far as your self is concerned, a little spiritual experience goes a long way. You are happy to leave all that other-worldly and imaginative talk to others, and prefer to stick with plain and simple facts.

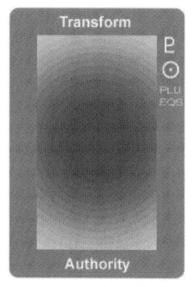

Pluto in the Plane of Sun's Equator

Your whole sense of yourself is indistinguishable from some sort of control and use of power. Try as you might, it is natural for you to be always in the thick of things, making changes and working to transform whatever is ready to give way to change.

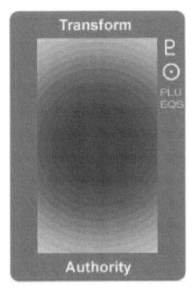

Pluto Square the Plane of Sun's Equator

Power and too-much control, in almost any form, is seldom appreciated by you. You go out of your way to avoid politics and the use of persuasion or force of any kind. You prefer to live without it.

The Mercury Plane

Venus in the Plane of Mercury

You have an inherent love of words and also have the gift to speak words of love. Mentally, you are a charmer, and your words speak volumes about how you care for all things bright and beautiful.

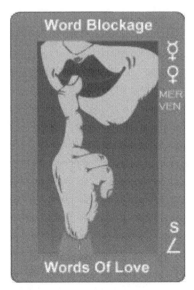

Venus Square the Plane of Mercury

You don't go for words and ideas that are somehow too fine and "nice." You like your thoughts neat and to the point. Words that are just too charming for everyday life, you avoid.

Interface: Planetary Nodes

Earth in the Plane of Mercury

Your mind and the way you use it is so much a part of your sense of self that the two are inseparable. The light in your eyes/mind is how others see your self.

Earth Square the Plane of Mercury

The way you see yourself is as not overly mental, not depending on wit and word-play to get across who you are and what you are all about.

Mars in the Plane of Mercury

Your mind seems always filled with energy, and you have the mental drive to push forward and accomplish. Mentally, you may appear too emotional from time to time, but this makes for a good speaker and projector of thoughts and ideas.

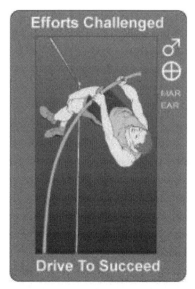

Mars Square the Plane of Mercury

Your mind may frequently be at odds with your emotions and your thoughts disconnected from what you really feel. You could lack the energy and drive to think things through.

Jupiter in the Plane of Mercury

Your mind is ever career-oriented and you probably a great problem solver and use your mind as part of how you make a living. You could make a good counselor or guide for others.

Jupiter Square the Plane of Mercury

Your own thoughts and what you think may often by at cross-purposes with your career moves, how you go about making a living. You may have trouble seeking guidance and taking needed vocational advice.

Ideas Of Discipline

Disciplined Mind

Saturn in the Plane of Mercury

When it comes to thoughts and thinking them, you are naturally disciplined and very organized. Perhaps it could be said that you run too much to the serious side, but no one can question your sincerity and dedication.

Saturn Square the Plane of Mercury

You are mentally light-hearted and like to keep it that way. Thoughts which are too serious or confining are not your cup of tea, and you refuse to let things get too solemn for too long.

Uranus in the Plane of Mercury

An unusual mind, unusual thoughts and ideas, and perhaps unconventional with and wordplay can be said to be earmarks of who you are. You love whatever gets your mind out of the box and into fee space.

Uranus Square the Plane of Mercury

Your mind goes against the unconventional and the eccentric and feels at home fitting in and conforming. No need for wild and crazy ideas, when the tried and the true are just that for a very good reason - they work best.

Neptune in the Plane of Mercury

You thoughts and mental machinations frequently have an other-worldly quality about them, and can be inspired and very creative. You may find a voice for this gift through music, speaking, acting, and theater. Spiritual ideas are natural for you.

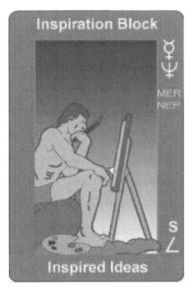

Neptune Square the Plane of Mercury

Not overly given to creative fantasy or mental flights of the imagination, you prefer to think things through in a more practical manner. You probably don't think out-of-the-box a whole lot.

Pluto in the Plane of Mercury

You can be a powerful thinker, with a strong control over what you think and say. On the other hand, the flip side of this is that you can be too controlling or your thoughts run to questions of control and power.

Pluto Square the Plane of Mercury

You are not mentally comfortable with too much change or coming up against control and power issues. You choose not to go there.

The Venus Plane

Mercury in the Plane of Venus

You have an inherent love of words and also have the gift to speak words of love. Mentally, you are a charmer, and your words speak volumes about how you care for all things bright and beautiful.

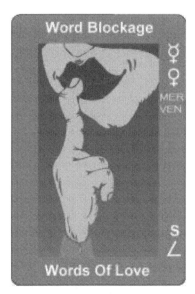

Mercury Square the Plane of Venus

You don't go for words and ideas that are somehow too fine and "nice." You like your thoughts neat and to the point. Words that are just too charming for everyday life, you avoid.

Interface: Planetary Nodes

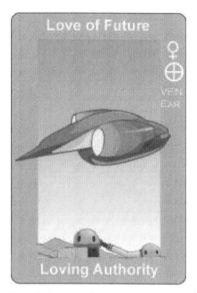

Earth in the Plane of Venus

This does not have to be as bad as it may sound, but your naturally just love yourself and this is plain for all to see. Might as well make it a virtue, for it is not about to go away or be hidden. Others may even take a lesson from you on self-appreciation.

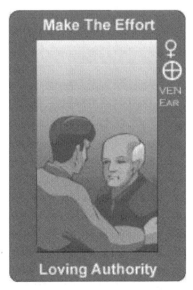

Earth Square the Plane of Venus

Your natural sense of yourself may be unappreciative or at least not able to appreciate and enjoy yourself as much as you might wish. If you follow your obvious self interests, you may mist a lot in life that others appear to enjoy.

Mars in the Plane of Venus

You naturally love action and adventure, ever driving and pushing forward whatever is at hand. Your love of energetic activity, sports and the outdoors amount to a life passion.

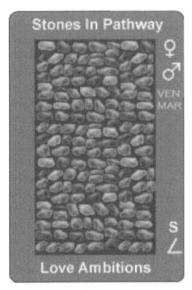

Mars Square the Plane of Venus

You can be a little indolent, and may not naturally be attracted to or care much about sports, exercise, getting outdoors, and generally pushing yourself in any way. You don't like it.

Interface: Planetary Nodes

Jupiter in the Plane of Venus

Your natural sense of appreciation and love may well amount to a career in your case. The critic or appraiser, the lover and enjoyer in you amounts to an avocation if not your vocation itself.

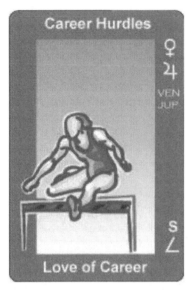

Jupiter Square the Plane of Venus

Your wish and tendency to enjoy yourself may sometimes be at the expense of your career and own best interests. It is an enigma to you why your own career suffers due to your penchant for venality.

Saturn in the Plane of Venus

Let's face it, you naturally love hard work and discipline. In fact you find the rules and regulations make it easier for your accomplish and apply yourse. You reverence of authority in almost a natural wonder.

Saturn Square the Plane of Venus

You don't care much for any kind of applied discipline, and rules and regulations are also out, as far as you are concerned. You don't like authorities of any kind and have little reverence for age or history.

Uranus in the Plane of Venus

You just naturally love whatever is different and unusual if for no other reason that it is unconventional. You love what is original and rebellious in yourself or anyone else. Whatever is normal, conventional, and conforming does not appeal to you.

Uranus Square the Plane of Venus

You like things neat and conventional, and the middle road is perfect as far as you are concerned. You seldom test the outer edges and fringe of life, and abhor rebels and eccentrics. The straight and narrow is fine with you.

Neptune in the Plane of Venus

You love whatever is fantastic and out-of-this-world, and music, film, theater, poetry and the like are as natural to you as a duck to water. This equally extends to all things spiritual and magical, whatever is transcendent and imaginative. You appreciate this.

117

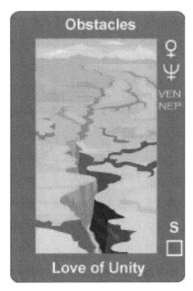

Neptune Square the Plane of Venus

Your natural sensitivities, what you like and tend to appreciate do not extend to anything you feel is unrealistic, and the so-called ideal is for you just another pipedream folks get lost in. You are hard-nosed when it comes to being realistic.

118

Pluto in the Plane of Venus

Others already know what you will have to admit, that you love power, intrigue, and being in control, whether in politics, business, or what-have-you? Some love diamonds and rubies. You love change, transformation, and occasionally turning the applecart upside down.

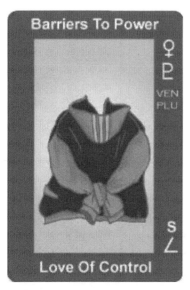

Barriers To Power

Love Of Control

Pluto Square the Plane of Venus

One thing you don't appreciate is politics, the misused of power, and any attempt to change the status quo by force or coercion. These you don't care for and are your avowed natural enemies.

The Earth Plane

Mercury in the Plane of Earth

Your mind and the way you use it is so much a part of your sense of self that the two are inseparable. The light in your eyes/mind is how others see your self.

Mercury Square the Plane of Earth

The way you see yourself is as not overly mental, not depending on wit and word-play to get across who you are and what you are all about.

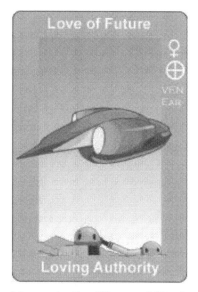

Venus in the Plane of Earth

This does not have to be as bad as it may sound, but your naturally just love yourself and this is plain for all to see. Might as well make it a virtue, for it is not about to go away or be hidden. Others may even take a lesson from you on self-appreciation.

Venus Square the Plane of Earth

Your natural sense of yourself may be unappreciative or at least not able to appreciate and enjoy yourself as much as you might wish. If you follow your obvious self interests, you may mist a lot in life that others appear to enjoy.

Mars in the Plane of Earth

The is always a bit of the "daring do" about you, and your tend to prefer to take risks than to avoid them. This permeates your whole sense of your self and you may love adventure and moving on.

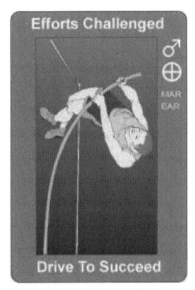

Mars Square the Plane of Earth

You tend not to push when it comes to shove, but prefer a more understated and less risky approach to life. It may take you time to find a life partner and settle down to a marriage.

Jupiter in the Plane of Earth

Deeply identifying with the career or avocation, perhaps even serving as a guide for others. Able to solve real problems.

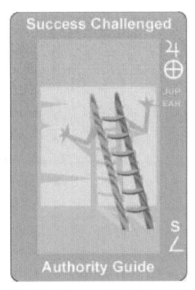

Jupiter Square the Plane of Earth

Trouble perhaps finding and identifying with one's career, perhaps even needing guidance in this area of life. Having problems finding the right way to go through life. Difficult solving life's puzzles.

Saturn in the Plane of Earth

You are naturally disciplined, organized, and your own slave driver. You know how to put the pedal to the metal, and concentrate on whatever you are doing light a single laser beam.

Saturn Square the Plane of Earth

You naturally avoid the rules, challenge authority, and try to get around regulations whenever you can. Your powers of organization, discipline, and concentration may be minimal.

Uranus in the Plane of Earth

You may feel that you are a born revolutionary, not cut from common cloth, but always riding the razor's edge of nonconformity, pushing the envelope. Your sense of yourself naturally does not choose the normal route, but always the road less travelled.

Uranus Square the Plane of Earth

You prefer the middle of the road in how you suit yourself, and would rather conform than deviate from conventionality. It is just the way you are. What is eccentric or non-usual is, for you, just out-of-bounds.

Neptune in the Plane of Earth

You are, if nothing else, somewhat other worldly, at home in the imaginative world of the imagination. Music, film, art, and anything that transcends and embraces the ordinary is just your cup of tea.

Neptune Square the Plane of Earth

You are not that into ideas of the "spiritual" and overly-refined flights of fancy and the imagination are something you probably avoid on principle. You are "in here," rather than somewhere "out there."

Ideas Transform

Transformation

Pluto in the Plane of Earth

You are a powerful one, that's for sure, and probably not without an explosion or two from time to time. You are at home with power and know how to use it. Control of one type or another is just natural to you.

Pluto Square the Plane of Earth

You don't like controlling or being controlled, and will go well out of your way to make sure it's not around. You like your own changes to come in a natural and unforced manner, and love of power is not something you condone or put up with.

The Mars Plane

Mercury in the Plane of Mars

Your mind seems always filled with energy, and you have the mental drive to push forward and accomplish. Mentally, you may appear too emotional from time to time, but this makes for a good speaker and projector of thoughts and ideas.

Mercury Square the Plane of Mars

Your mind may frequently be at odds with your emotions and your thoughts disconnected from what you really feel. You could lack the energy and drive to think things through.

Interface: Planetary Nodes

Venus in the Plane of Mars

You naturally love action and adventure, ever driving and pushing forward whatever is at hand. Your love of energetic activity, sports and the outdoors amount to a life passion.

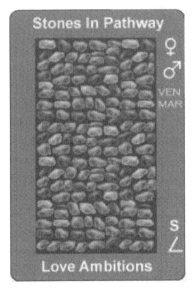

Venus Square the Plane of Mars

You can be a little indolent, and may not naturally be attracted to or care much about sports, exercise, getting outdoors, and generally pushing yourself in any way. You don't like it.

Ideas For Effort

♂

⊕

MAR
EAR

Drive To Succeed

Earth in the Plane of Mars

The is always a bit of the "daring do" about you, and your tend to prefer to take risks than to avoid them. This permeates your whole sense of your self and you may love adventure and moving on.

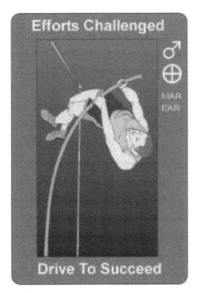

Earth Square the Plane of Mars

You tend not to push when it comes to shove, but prefer a more understated and less risky approach to life. It may take you time to find a life partner and settle down to a marriage.

Jupiter in the Plane of Mars

Your career drive and push may be unusually strong, and just about everything you attempt to do probably turns into something of an opportunity. You are career centered.

Jupiter Square the Plane of Mars

What you feel like doing and what might be a good career move for you may as often as not be at odds. Your drive to accomplish runs at right angles to what might be the best solution for you, the actual way to go.

Saturn in the Plane of Mars

With you, push come to shove may come too easily, and you can find yourself on the hard end of shovel once in a while. What can be a drive against authority and the rules on your part, if taken more slowly and evenly, can turn into something more like an engine of organization and control.

Saturn Square the Plane of Mars

You impulses can tend to be confrontational, in particular when it comes to following the rules and authorities in general. You don't like to be pinned down or hemmed in and push comes to shove pretty quickly with you.

Uranus in the Plane of Mars

You have an unusual drive and are probably driven to do some unusual things on top of that. A push or urge on your part to be original and unconventional may see you taking roads less travelled by. Possibly eccentric.

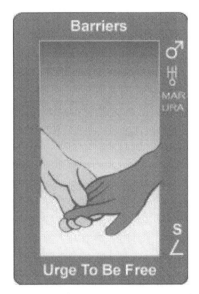

Uranus Square the Plane of Mars

You are conventional, rather than unconventional, and probably have an innate urge to avoid the eccentric and simply to conform. You are driven to uniformity just as some are driven to be different.

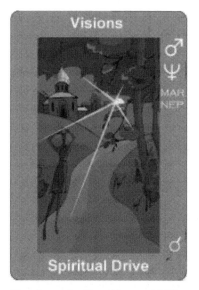

Neptune in the Plane of Mars

Your feelings are strong and always have a flair for the dramatic, which could be perfect if you are a musician or an actor. Spiritual directions are also empowered here. You feel in a grand way, and these feelings power your imagination and can be inspirational to others.

Neptune Square the Plane of Mars

You may have difficulty feeling inspired at times, and even go out of your way to avoid escape or even entertainment. You manage to stay away from big-picture ideas, spirituality, and the life.

Pluto in the Plane of Mars

It could be said that you find trouble easily, but what really is at issue here is your drive to change or transform things can often turn into a an attempt to control or hang on to power. You may have to learn to tread more gently with your feelings.

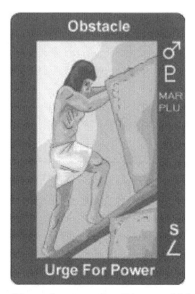

Pluto Square the Plane of Mars

Your natural drive and feelings may be such that you avoid confrontation, at least of a possibly transformative nature. You don't like to be controlled and change is something you like to take a step at a time.

The Jupiter Plane

Mercury in the Plane of Jupiter

Your mind is ever career-oriented and you probably a great problem solver and use your mind as part of how you make a living. You could make a good counselor or guide for others.

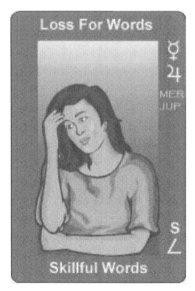

Mercury Square the Plane of Jupiter

Your own thoughts and what you think may often by at cross-purposes with your career moves, how you go about making a living. You may have trouble seeking guidance and taking needed vocational advice.

Venus in the Plane of Jupiter

Your natural sense of appreciation and love may well amount to a career in your case. The critic or appraiser, the lover and enjoyer in you amounts to an avocation if not your vocation itself.

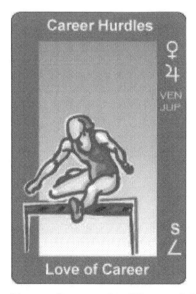

Venus Square the Plane of Jupiter

Your wish and tendency to enjoy yourself may sometimes be at the expense of your career and own best interests. It is an enigma to you why your own career suffers due to your penchant for venality.

Earth in the Plane of Jupiter

Deeply identifying with the career or avocation, perhaps even serving as a guide for others. Able to solve real problems.

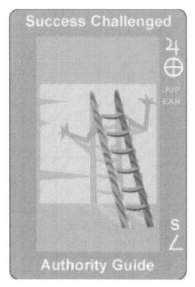

Earth Square the Plane of Jupiter

Trouble perhaps finding and identifying with one's career, perhaps even needing guidance in this area of life. Having problems finding the right way to go through life. Difficult solving life's puzzles.

Interface: Planetary Nodes

Mars in the Plane of Jupiter

Your career drive and push may be unusually strong, and just about everything you attempt to do probably turns into something of an opportunity. You are career centered.

Mars Square the Plane of Jupiter

What you feel like doing and what might be a good career move for you may as often as not be at odds. Your drive to accomplish runs at right angles to what might be the best solution for you, the actual way to go.

Interface: Planetary Nodes

Saturn in the Plane of Jupiter

You may choose a highly disciplined career, one filled with hard work and a real organized approach to life. Your life path is serious business.

Saturn Square the Plane of Jupiter

In your career and way through life, you may tend to buck authority and be less disciplined that the average, preferring to find ways around the rules rather than follow them.

Uranus in the Plane of Jupiter

You may choose an unusual career or at least bring a flair for the unusual and unconventional to whatever you do for a living. You definitely chose the road less traveled by.

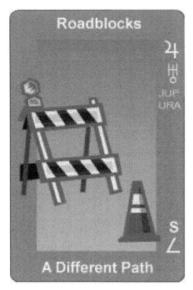

Uranus Square the Plane of Jupiter

You prefer a simple straight-forward career to one more unconventional. When it comes to your particular life path, you enjoy the straight and narrow and tend to avoid what is eccentric and unusual.

Neptune in the Plane of Jupiter

A career with a certain added glamour or inspiration. This could point to working with music or film, but also to spiritual areas and creative imagination. Treading the way of compassion.

Interface: Planetary Nodes

Neptune Square the Plane of Jupiter

A career or path that is simple and direct, with little interest glamour and grand ideas. There could be an avoidance of spiritual topics, little fanfare, and keeping the nose to the grindstone.

Pluto in the Plane of Jupiter

You may find that it is through your career that real change come about, change that is transformative and life-changing. Also choosing a way through life that requires real control or flirts with power, politics, and the like.

Pluto Square the Plane of Jupiter

You may tend to avoid confrontation and the powerful, preferring a more simple path. Change and personal transformation may be something you tend to avoid in favor of regularity and uniformity.

The Saturn Plane

Mercury in the Plane of Saturn

When it comes to thoughts and thinking them, you are naturally disciplined and very organized. Perhaps it could be said that you run too much to the serious side, but no one can question your sincerity and dedication.

Mercury Square the Plane of Saturn

You are mentally light-hearted and like to keep it that way. Thoughts which are too serious or confining are not your cup of tea, and you refuse to let things get too solemn for too long.

Venus in the Plane of Saturn

Let's face it, you naturally love hard work and discipline. In fact you find the rules and regulations make it easier for your accomplish and apply yourse. You reverence of authority in almost a natural wonder.

Venus Square the Plane of Saturn

You don't care much for any kind of applied discipline, and rules and regulations are also out, as far as you are concerned. You don't like authorities of any kind and have little reverence for age or history.

Ideas of Authority

Authority Figure

Earth in the Plane of Saturn

You are naturally disciplined, organized, and your own slave driver. You know how to put the pedal to the metal, and concentrate on whatever you are doing light a single laser beam.

Earth Square the Plane of Saturn

You naturally avoid the rules, challenge authority, and try to get around regulations whenever you can. Your powers of organization, discipline, and concentration may be minimal.

Mars in the Plane of Saturn

With you, push come to shove may come too easily, and you can find yourself on the hard end of shovel once in a while. What can be a drive against authority and the rules on your part, if taken more slowly and evenly, can turn into something more like an engine of organization and control.

Mars Square the Plane of Saturn

You impulses can tend to be confrontational, in particular when it comes to following the rules and authorities in general. You don't like to be pinned down or hemmed in and push comes to shove pretty quickly with you.

Jupiter in the Plane of Saturn

You may choose a highly disciplined career, one filled with hard work and a real organized approach to life. Your life path is serious business.

Jupiter Square the Plane of Saturn

In your career and way through life, you may tend to buck authority and be less disciplined that the average, preferring to find ways around the rules rather than follow them.

Interface: Planetary Nodes

Uranus in the Plane of Saturn

You natural sense of discipline and hard work is enhanced by a strong streak of inventiveness and sheer insight. You can see how to use things, whatever is a fact, to best advantage, often coming up with new uses for old objects.

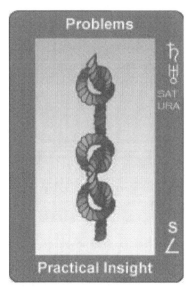

Uranus Square the Plane of Saturn

Your hard-working ethic and natural sense of discipline follows a very conventional path, and while not very inventive, manages to get the job done. You may tend to view what is unconventional or eccentric with a cautious eye.

Neptune in the Plane of Saturn

Your natural sense of order and discipline always seems to have something other worldly or spiritual about it, and to serve a greater use of function. You bring acceptance of hard work as a just a part of life.

Neptune Square the Plane of Saturn

Your natural sense of hard work can't help by rail against the world of the creative imagination, not because these two are incompatible, but it is just how you feel.

Pluto in the Plane of Saturn

You are indeed concentrated and discipline, and this is natural to you. However, you also have a flair for being a bit of a control freak and going over the top in wielding power and administering punishment. You may have to become aware of this.

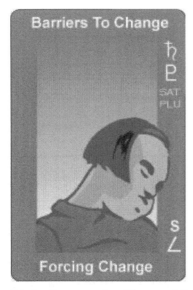

Pluto Square the Plane of Saturn

I hard-work ethic and natural sense of organization does not extend to the overuse of power, over politicizing of situations, and attempts to control others. These are your natural enemies.

The Uranus Plane

Mercury in the Plane of Uranus

An unusual mind, unusual thoughts and ideas, and perhaps unconventional with and wordplay can be said to be earmarks of who you are. You love whatever gets your mind out of the box and into fee space.

Mercury Square the Plane of Uranus

Your mind goes against the unconventional and the eccentric and feels at home fitting in and conforming. No need for wild and crazy ideas, when the tried and the true are just that for a very good reason - they work best.

Venus in the Plane of Uranus

You just naturally love whatever is different and unusual if for no other reason that it is unconventional. You love what is original and rebellious in yourself or anyone else. Whatever is normal, conventional, and conforming does not appeal to you.

Venus Square the Plane of Uranus

You like things neat and conventional, and the middle road is perfect as far as you are concerned. You seldom test the outer edges and fringe of life, and abhor rebels and eccentrics. The straight and narrow is fine with you.

Earth in the Plane of Uranus

You may feel that you are a born revolutionary, not cut from common cloth, but always riding the razor's edge of nonconformity, pushing the envelope. Your sense of yourself naturally does not choose the normal route, but always the road less travelled.

Earth Square the Plane of Uranus

You prefer the middle of the road in how you suit yourself, and would rather conform than deviate from conventionality. It is just the way you are. What is eccentric or non-usual is, for you, just out-of-bounds.

Mars in the Plane of Uranus

You have an unusual drive and are probably driven to do some unusual things on top of that. A push or urge on your part to be original and unconventional may see you taking roads less travelled by. Possibly eccentric.

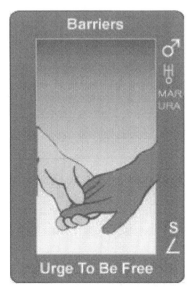

Mars Square the Plane of Uranus

You are conventional, rather than unconventional, and probably have an innate urge to avoid the eccentric and simply to conform. You are driven to uniformity just as some are driven to be different.

Jupiter in the Plane of Uranus

You may choose an unusual career or at least bring a flair for the unusual and unconventional to whatever you do for a living. You definitely chose the road less traveled by.

193

Jupiter Square the Plane of Uranus

You prefer a simple straight-forward career to one more unconventional. When it comes to your particular life path, you enjoy the straight and narrow and tend to avoid what is eccentric and unusual.

Interface: Planetary Nodes

Saturn in the Plane of Uranus

You natural sense of discipline and hard work is enhanced by a strong streak of inventiveness and sheer insight. You can see how to use things, whatever is a fact, to best advantage, often coming up with new uses for old objects.

Interface: Planetary Nodes

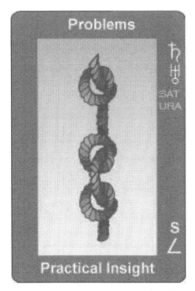

Saturn Square the Plane of Uranus

Your hard-working ethic and natural sense of discipline follows a very conventional path, and while not very inventive, manages to get the job done. You may tend to view what is unconventional or eccentric with a cautious eye.

Interface: Planetary Nodes

Neptune in the Plane of Uranus

You have a naturally inventive way of doing things, but one that is not eccentric for eccentricity's sake, but rather always manages to pull a situation together, and to bring unity out of chaos.

Neptune Square the Plane of Uranus

Your love of eccentricity and the unconventional delights in railing against the more conventional, concentric, what you might call the "Peacemakers." You like it edgy and unpredictable, and don't mind sharing your opinion.

Interface: Planetary Nodes

Pluto in the Plane of Uranus

Your natural rebelliousness and love of the unconventional verges on the problematical, due to a tendency to resort to force and even a little coercion to see things done your way. You are inventive and perhaps even original, but a bully is bully nevertheless.

Pluto Square the Plane of Uranus

You like to see yourself as original, inventive, and a bit of a rebel, at the very least unconventional and non-conformist. You have made the brokers of power and the bullies of the world your natural enemy and will leave no stone unturned in letting them know how you feel.

The Neptune Plane

Mercury in the Plane of Neptune

You thoughts and mental machinations frequently have an other-worldly quality about them, and can be inspired and very creative. You may find a voice for this gift through music, speaking, acting, and theater. Spiritual ideas are natural for you.

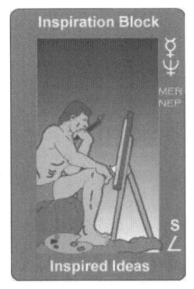

Mercury Square the Plane of Neptune

Not overly given to creative fantasy or mental flights of the imagination, you prefer to think things through in a more practical manner. You probably don't think out-of-the-box a whole lot.

Venus in the Plane of Neptune

You love whatever is fantastic and out-of-this-world, and music, film, theater, poetry and the like are as natural to you as a duck to water. This equally extends to all things spiritual and magical, whatever is transcendent and imaginative. You appreciate this.

Venus Square the Plane of Neptune

Your natural sensitivities, what you like and tend to appreciate do not extend to anything you feel is unrealistic, and the so-called ideal is for you just another pipedream folks get lost in. You are hard-nosed when it comes to being realistic.

Earth in the Plane of Neptune

You are, if nothing else, somewhat other worldly, at home in the imaginative world of the imagination. Music, film, art, and anything that transcends and embraces the ordinary is just your cup of tea.

Earth Square the Plane of Neptune

You are not that into ideas of the "spiritual" and overly-refined flights of fancy and the imagination are something you probably avoid on principle. You are "in here," rather than somewhere "out there."

Interface: Planetary Nodes

Mars in the Plane of Neptune

Your feelings are strong and always have a flair for the dramatic, which could be perfect if you are a musician or an actor. Spiritual directions are also empowered here. You feel in a grand way, and these feelings power your imagination and can be inspirational to others.

Mars Square the Plane of Neptune

You may have difficulty feeling inspired at times, and even go out of your way to avoid escape or even entertainment. You manage to stay away from big-picture ideas, spirituality, and the life.

Jupiter in the Plane of Neptune

A career with a certain added glamour or inspiration. This could point to working with music or film, but also to spiritual areas and creative imagination. Treading the way of compassion.

Jupiter Square the Plane of Neptune

A career or path that is simple and direct, with little interest glamour and grand ideas. There could be an avoidance of spiritual topics, little fanfare, and keeping the nose to the grindstone.

Saturn in the Plane of Neptune

Your natural sense of order and discipline always seems to have something other worldly or spiritual about it, and to serve a greater use of function. You bring acceptance of hard work as a just a part of life.

Saturn Square the Plane of Neptune

Your natural sense of hard work can't help by rail against the world of the creative imagination, not because these two are incompatible, but it is just how you feel.

Uranus in the Plane of Neptune

You have a naturally inventive way of doing things, but one that is not eccentric for eccentricity's sake, but rather always manages to pull a situation together, and to bring unity out of chaos.

Uranus Square the Plane of Neptune

Your love of eccentricity and the unconventional delights in railing against the more conventional, concentric, what you might call the "Peacemakers." You like it edgy and unpredictable, and don't mind sharing your opinion.

Interface: Planetary Nodes

Pluto in the Plane of Neptune

Your natural inclination toward the mystical and otherworldly goes a little bit farther than most, venturing into whatever is transformative and consciousness changing. You believe in compassion and acceptance, but almost with a vengeance. Could make for good skills with music and the theater.

Pluto Square the Plane of Neptune

Your sense of togetherness of simple acceptance is well within the bounds of convention. All these things should happen naturally and force, of even the slightest kind, should never be used.

The Pluto Plane

Mercury in the Plane of Pluto

You can be a powerful thinker, with a strong control over what you think and say. On the other hand, the flip side of this is that you can be too controlling or your thoughts run to questions of control and power.

Mercury Square the Plane of Pluto

You are not mentally comfortable with too much change or coming up against control and power issues. You choose not to go there.

Interface: Planetary Nodes

Venus in the Plane of Pluto

Others already know what you will have to admit, that you love power, intrigue, and being in control, whether in politics, business, or what-have-you? Some love diamonds and rubies. You love change, transformation, and occasionally turning the applecart upside down.

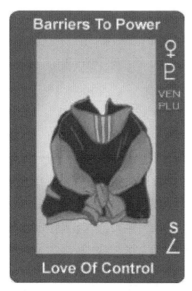

Venus Square the Plane of Pluto

One thing you don't appreciate is politics, the misused of power, and any attempt to change the status quo by force or coercion. These you don't care for and are your avowed natural enemies.

Earth in the Plane of Pluto

You are a powerful one, that's for sure, and probably not without an explosion or two from time to time. You are at home with power and know how to use it. Control of one type or another is just natural to you.

Earth Square the Plane of Pluto

You don't like controlling or being controlled, and will go well out of your way to make sure it's not around. You like your own changes to come in a natural and unforced manner, and love of power is not something you condone or put up with.

Mars in the Plane of Pluto

It could be said that you find trouble easily, but what really is at issue here is your drive to change or transform things can often turn into a an attempt to control or hang on to power. You may have to learn to tread more gently with your feelings.

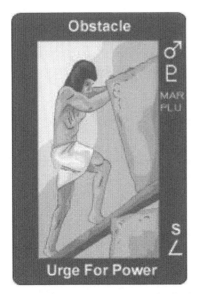

Mars Square the Plane of Pluto

Your natural drive and feelings may be such that you avoid confrontation, at least of a possibly transformative nature. You don't like to be controlled and change is something you like to take a step at a time.

Interface: Planetary Nodes

Jupiter in the Plane of Pluto

You may find that it is through your career that real change come about, change that is transformative and life-changing. Also choosing a way through life that requires real control or flirts with power, politics, and the like.

Jupiter Square the Plane of Pluto

You may tend to avoid confrontation and the powerful, preferring a more simple path. Change and personal transformation may be something you tend to avoid in favor of regularity and uniformity.

Saturn in the Plane of Pluto

You are indeed concentrated and discipline, and this is natural to you. However, you also have a flair for being a bit of a control freak and going over the top in wielding power and administering punishment. You may have to become aware of this.

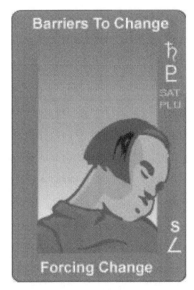

Saturn Square the Plane of Pluto

I hard-work ethic and natural sense of organization does not extend to the overuse of power, over politicizing of situations, and attempts to control others. These are your natural enemies.

Uranus in the Plane of Pluto

Your natural rebelliousness and love of the unconventional verges on the problematical, due to a tendency to resort to force and even a little coercion to see things done your way. You are inventive and perhaps even original, but a bully is bully nevertheless.

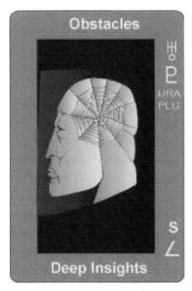

Uranus Square the Plane of Pluto

You like to see yourself as original, inventive, and a bit of a rebel, at the very least unconventional and non-conformist. You have made the brokers of power and the bullies of the world your natural enemy and will leave no stone unturned in letting them know how you feel.

Interface: Planetary Nodes

Neptune in the Plane of Pluto

Your natural inclination toward the mystical and otherworldly goes a little bit farther than most, venturing into whatever is transformative and consciousness changing. You believe in compassion and acceptance, but almost with a vengeance. Could make for good skills with music and the theater.

Neptune Square the Plane of Pluto

Your sense of togetherness of simple acceptance is well within the bounds of convention. All these things should happen naturally and force, of even the slightest kind, should never be used.

The Invariable Plane

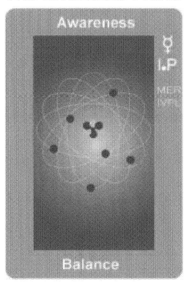

Mercury in the Plane of Invariable Plane

Your mind is very stable and you are not easily knocked off point in a conversation. It is like you have the weight of the universe behind what you think and say.

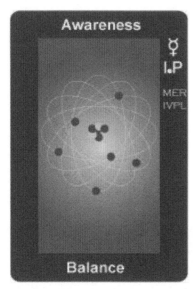

Mercury Square the Plane of Invariable Plane

Your with and mind may not be as stable as you might wish and may find thinking tough at times or feel that you are tilting at mental windmills from time to time.

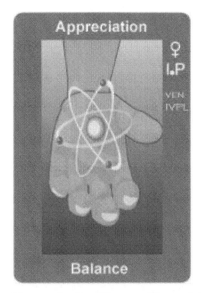

Venus in the Plane of Invariable Plane

A lover, an admirer of others and life, an appreciator of just about everyone and everything, this sense of what some might call venality is as natural to you as waves on an ocean. Don't even try to change. It is something like a mandate to enjoy.

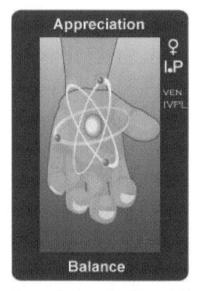

Venus Square the Plane of Invariable Plane

You attempts to enjoy and love lift often appear to be at odds with life itself, always either a day late and a dollar short or some such nonsense. Whatever the cause, you often can't seem to enjoy as much as you would like of life.

Interface: Planetary Nodes

Earth in the Plane of Invariable Plane

A very stable and steady sense of the self and where you are going. Not easily disturbed or pushed off course.

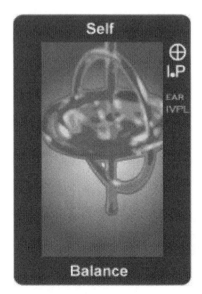

Earth Square the Plane of Invariable Plane

A somewhat unstable and unsteady sense of the self and where you are going, the future. Can be easily disturbed or pushed off course.

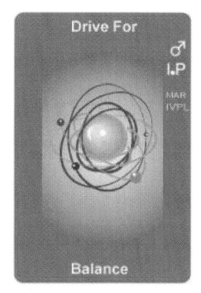

\Mars in the Plane of Invariable Plane

Some will find you sense of adventure and the way you come on somewhat larger than life, and you can appear as an intimidating figure with your innate sense of 'daring-do."

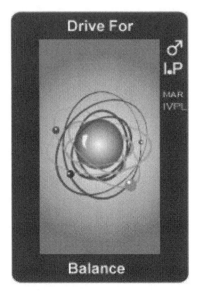

Mars Square the Plane of Invariable Plane

Your drive to accomplish and get things done may fall short on occasion, and feel that the universe is sometimes not all-the-way behind you, not backing you up. You may lack a certain oomph.

Interface: Planetary Nodes

Jupiter in the Plane of Invariable Plane

Career stable beyond average expectations. Rock certainty in finding one's way through the obstacles of life, able to easily solving problems, and probably able to lead others as well.

Way of

♃
I.P

JUP
IVPL

Balance

Jupiter Square the Plane of Invariable Plane

Career perhaps more unstable than on average. A tendency to go against the tide or grain. You may require help or guidance in this area.

Interface: Planetary Nodes

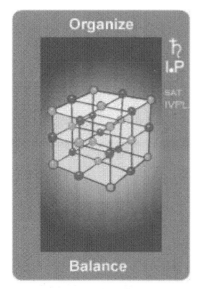

Saturn in the Plane of Invariable Plane

Like a stone or part of the natural universe, discipline, hard work, and concentration are as much a part of you as waves on the ocean. You are a born worker.

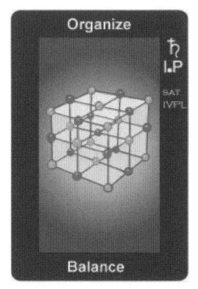

Saturn Square the Plane of Invariable Plane

You can't seem to help going against authority or whatever the natural order of things are, and this kind of attitude will not get far, without some modification.

Interface: Planetary Nodes

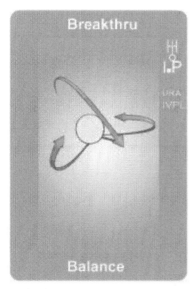

Uranus in the Plane of Invariable Plane

A natural rebel is for you the norm, and those who come to know you will agree: on you the eccentric looks pretty normal. This is no act you are putting on, but like a suit of clothes tailor-made for you, everything extraordinary and cutting-edge is where you are most yourself.

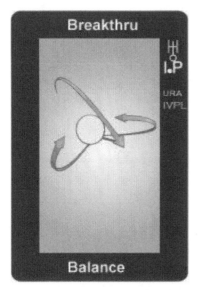

Uranus Square the Plane of Invariable Plane

In large part, your unconventionality and insistence on doing things differently or in a non-standard fashion gets you nowhere. This radical streak goes against the grain of conventionality and will bring you few rewards.

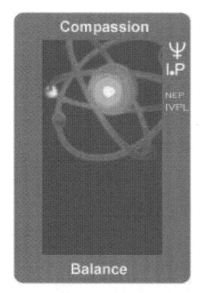

Neptune in the Plane of Invariable Plane

Spiritual values, compassion, and always taking the larger view of things are not only natural to you, but are a pretty-much unshakable part of who you know yourself to be. This could also involve music, film, and the arts.

Interface: Planetary Nodes

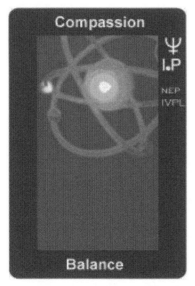

Neptune Square the Plane of Invariable Plane

The whole question of spirituality, flights of the imagination, and all of that "way out there" stuff is probably just not your cup of tea. You believe in brotherly love, but probably more on a bootstrap basis, every man or woman getting on his or her own feet.

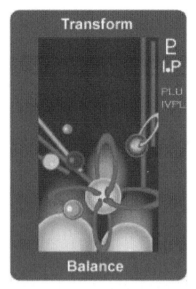

Pluto in the Plane of Invariable Plane

You are not one to mess with, at least not when it comes to holding, using, or abusing power. You are as natural in that area is sunlight in the daytime. Although others have the kind of control you enjoy, few have such an obvious mandate to use it.

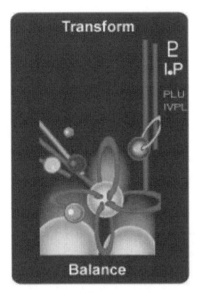

Pluto Square the Plane of Invariable Plane

You are no friend of those who coerce or wield power, much less abuse it. Change or transformation may come in time, but it is not something you court or seek out.

Interface: Planetary Nodes

Technical Data

Inclinations Ordered on Ecliptic

The ascending nodes are ordered by their position on the Earth's ecliptic plane.

MERCURY 0 47.145944° + 4266.75"T + 0.626T2+1.18528°T

MARS 0 48.786442° + 2775.57"T - 0.005"T2-0.0192"T3+0.77111°T

URANUS 073.489903° + 1838.25"T+0.49889°T

SUN'S EQUATOR 074.366667° + 5040.0"T+1.40000"T

VENUS 0 75.779647° + 3239.46"T + 1.476"T2+0.89972°T

JUPITER 099.437861° + 3639.5"T+1.0I083°T

INVARIABLE PLANE 106.583611° + 3452.0"T+0.95888°T

PLUTO 109.683462° + 5400.0"T+1.50000°T

SATURN 112.783567° + 3143.43"T+0.87278°T

NEPTUNE 130.678689° + 3966.54"T+1.09833°T

Interface: Planetary Nodes

Inclinations and Ascending Nodes

Ordered Relative to Ascending Node on Ecliptic

MERCURY
07.0028806° + 06.699"T -0.066"T2

MARS
01.8503333° - 02.43"T +0.0454"T2

URANUS
00.7727222° + 02.00"T

SUN'S EQUATOR
07.25°

VENUS
03.3936306° + 03.621"T -0.0035"T2

JUPITER
01.3086944° - 20.0"T

INVARIABLE PLANE
01.5830556° - 18.0"T

PLUTO
17.1698661°

SATURN
02.4925833° - 16.0"T

NEPTUNE
01.7792499° - 33.0"T

Note: The above epoch for 1900, January 0.5 ET or Julian Day 2415020.0. The time interval from the epoch is denoted by T and is measured in Julian centuries of 36525 ephemeris days. All elements are the MEAN elements for above epoch except elements for Pluto which are osculating elements at the epoch 1950.0 or JED 2433282.423. See note above on Pluto.

Interface: Planetary Nodes

Pluto: The orbit of Pluto is still being defined. For purposes of this book it was necessary to select an approximate value for pluto's motion in a Julian century of 36525 days. The above value was selected although one should realize that this is only an approximation, good to within perhaps a degree of the value listed.

Inclinations Ordered

EPOCH 1900.0 (all values this page). Inclinations. Ordered Relative to the Plane of the Earth 12345

Planet	#1	#2	#3	#4
PLUTO	17.2°	Sun	Earth	Uranus
EQUATOR SUN	07.3	Mercury	Pluto	Earth
MERCURY	07.0	Sun	Pluto	Neptune
VENUS	03.4	Mars	Pluto	Mercury
SATURN	02.5	I-plane	Pluto	Mercury
MARS	01.9	Uranus	Pluto	Sun
NEPTUNE	01.8	I-plane	Pluto	Mercury
INVAR.PLANE	01.6	Jupiter	Pluto	Mercury
JUPITER	01.3	I-plane	Pluto	Mercury}
URANUS	00.8	Jupiter	Pluto	Sun
EARTH	00.0	Uranus	Pluto	Sun

Above Columns:

#1. Different in inclination of planet and Earth's plane.

#2 Planet to which listed planet is most mutually inclined.

253

Interface: Planetary Nodes

#3. Planet to which listed planet is Least mutually inclined.

#4 Pluto aside, least mutually inclined planet.

Interface: Planetary Nodes

Interface and Square Point Formulae

The following table represents the amount of change (in the direction of the zodiac signs, counterclockwise) that the Interface and each of the Square Points make in a Julian Century of 365.25 days. They would be of use in calculating the approximate position of the various points for epochs not included among the tables in this book. For instance, the first on the list, the Interface Mercury-Mars (from the table 1900.0 elsewhere in this book) is 46.5607 degrees plus 1.33352 degrees per century advance. This amount is to be added for years after 1900.0 and subtracted for years prior to 1900.0.

INTERFACE	IF	SP-1	SP-2
mercury-mars	1.33352	1.33543	1.33410
mercury-uranus	1.25563	1.25663	1.25570
mercury-Sun	1.35723	1.35473	1.35778
mercury-venus	1.32612	1.32749	1.32579
mercury-jupiter	1.24959	1.25043	1.24963
mercury-I-plane	1.24932	1.25010	1.24923
mercury-pluto	1.51641	1.51158	1.51744
mercury-saturn	1.23909	1.23953	1.23843
mercury-neptune	1.25998	1.26085	1.25976
mars-uranus	0.87411	0.87422	0.87412
mars-Sun	1.56595	1.56624	1.56853
mars-venus	0.94634	0.94628	0.94650
mars-jupiter	0.99312	0.99314	0.99310
mars-I-plane	0.97558	0.97554	0.97547

Interface: Planetary Nodes

```
mars-pluto        1.52943 1.52887  1.53218
mars-saturn       0.90811 0.90801  0.90792
mars-neptune      1.08660 1.08659  1.08632
uranus-Sun        1.50559 1.50569  1.50808
uranus-venus      1.01518 1.01528  1.01564
uranus-jupiter    1.58331 1.58325  1.58336
uranus-I-plane    1.28076 1.28071  1.28082
uranus-pluto      1.53631 1.53635  1.53981
uranus-saturn     1.00323 1.00320  1.00335
uranus-neptune    1.30995 1.30981  1.30985
Sun-venus         1.83542 1.84245  1.83866
Sun-jupiter       1.49778 1.49935  1.49802
Sun-I-plane       1.51960 1.52146  1.51981
Sun-pluto         1.53338 1.53263  1.53575
Sun-saturn        1.57557 1.57707  1.57533
Sun-neptune       1.50486 1.50638  1.50476
venus-jupiter     0.94019 0.94029  0.94030
venus-I-plane     0.98782 0.98801  0.98795
venus-pluto       1.60418 1.60454  1.61376
venus-saturn      1.04765 1.04756  1.04737
venus-neptune     1.09119 1.09144  1.09123
jupiter-I-plane   0.64359 0.64341  0.64334
jupiter-pluto     1.53434 1.53453  1.53782
jupiter-saturn    0.67877 0.67856  0.67835
jupiter-neptune   1.20017 1.20004  1.19989
I-plane-pluto     1.55180 1.55219  1.55640
I-plane-saturn    0.69629 0.69605  0.69590
```

Interface: Planetary Nodes

```
I-plane-neptune  1.36744 1.36713  1.36707
pluto-saturn     1.60345 1.61334  1.60480
pluto-neptune    1.55333 1.55834  1.55384
saturn-neptune   0.89809 0.89829  0.89841
```

Basic Data for Epoch 1900.0: Part 1

Below is a table with the Interface data listed by planetary pair, followed by the position of the node on the Earth's ecliptic (second column), and with the first Square Point.

Interface: Planetary Nodes

	Interface	Square-1
mercury-mars	046.5607	136.5519
mercury-uranus	044.0525	134.0059
mercury-Sun	146.6179	236.4796
mercury-venus	025.2738	114.9755
mercury-jupiter	037.7196	127.5800
mercury-I/plane	034.8064	124.6260
mercury-pluto	133.0455	223.1063
mercury-saturn	026.4341	116.1487
mercury-neptune	032.6444	129.4350
mars-uranus	033.0860	123.0704
mars-Sun	082.4611	172.4887
mars-venus	101.4462	191.4750
mars-jupiter	004.0367	094.0068
mars-I-plane	175.7172	085.6885
mars-pluto	115.1813	205.2033
mars-saturn	157.4574	247.4330
mars-neptune	001.0265	090.9968
uranus-Sun	074.4706	164.4710
uranus-venus	076.4534	166.4540
uranus-jupiter	128.2772	218.2821
uranus-I/plane	130.8478	220.8526
uranus-pluto	111.2139	201.2190
uranus-saturn	127.2559	217.2609
uranus-neptune	156.1883	246.1896
Sun-venus	073.1336	163.1136
Sun-jupiter	069.1741	159.0905
Sun-I-plane	066.2905	156.1616
Sun-pluto	129.4036	219.8343
Sun-saturn	058.1673	147.9192
Sun-neptune	061.1419	150.9355
venus-jupiter	062.3441	152.2985
venus-I plane	054.0782	144.0090
venus-pluto	116.9404	207.0400
venus-saturn	028.9005	118.8001
venus-neptune	044.2577	134.1680

Interface: Planetary Nodes

	Interface	Square-1
jupiter-I plane	136.3489	226.3633
jupiter-pluto	110.4960	200.5017
jupiter-saturn	126.6866	216.6988
jupiter-neptune	176.4552	266.4618
I-plane-pluto	109.9878	199.9904
I-plane-saturn	123.3140	213.3261
I-plane-neptune	193.3314	283.3339
pluto-saturn	109.1754	199.1268
pluto-neptune	107.4070	197.1899
saturn-neptune	078.4410	168.3905

Basic Data for Epoch 1900.0: Part 2

Below is a table with the Interface data listed by planetary pair, followed by the position of the second Square Point (2nd column), and the degrees (and fractions of a degree of the node above or below the Earth's ecliptic (3rd column).

	SQUARE-2	IF:LAT
mercury-mars	136.5583	-0.0719
mercury-uranus	134.0481	-0.3798
mercury-Sun	236.8832	+6.9083
mercury-venus	115.1751	-2.6201
mercury-jupiter	127.7071	-1.1525
mercury-I/plane	124.7934	-1.5037
mercury-pluto	225.0065	+6.9851
mercury-saturn	116.4272	-2.4875
mercury-neptune	122.6520	-1.7618
mars-uranus	123.0809	-0.5009
mars-Sun	172.5904	+1.0262
mars-venus	191.5248	+1.4713
mars-jupiter	094.0395	-1.3019
mars-I-plane	085.7318	-1.4793
mars-pluto	205.7095	+1.6956
mars-saturn	247.5116	+1.7530
mars-neptune	091.0537	-1.3701
uranus-Sun	164.4722	+0.0132
uranus-venus	166.4558	+0.0400
uranus-jupiter	218.2898	+0.6313
uranus-I/plane	220.8642	+0.6507
uranus-pluto	201.3600	+0.4728
uranus-saturn	217.2822	+0.6233
uranus-neptune	246.2098	+0.7665
Sun-venus	163.1243	-0.1569
Sun-jupiter	159.1611	-0.6596
Sun-I-plane	156.2689	-1.0239
Sun-pluto	221.1218	+5.9519

Interface: Planetary Nodes

	SQUARE-2	IF:LAT
Sun-saturn	148.1161	-2.0326
Sun-neptune	151.1238	-1.6670
venus-jupiter	152.3297	-0.7894
venus-I plane	144.0571	-1.2561
venus-pluto	207.6247	+2.2351
venus-saturn	118.8890	-2.4734
venus-neptune	134.2543	-1.7758
jupiter-I plane	226.3678	+0.7861
jupiter-pluto	200.5736	+0.2511
jupiter-saturn	216.7119	+0.5993
jupiter-neptune	266.4829	+1.2753
I-plane-pluto	200.0140	+0.0940
I-plane-saturn	213.3335	+0.4558
I-plane-neptune	283.3540	+1.5805
pluto-saturn	199.1686	-0.1570
pluto-neptune	197.3869	-0.7032
saturn-neptune	168.4143	-1.4068

Interface: Planetary Nodes

Basic Data for Epoch 1900.0: Part 3

Below is a table with the Interface data listed by planetary pair, followed by the position of the first Square Point Latitude (2nd column), the position of the second Square Point Latitude (3rd column), and the angle.

	SQ1:LAT	SQ2:LAT	ANGLE
mercury-mars	+7.0025	+1.8489	5.1536
mercury-uranus	+6.9925	+0.6729	6.3197
mercury-Sun	-1.1413	+2.1888	3.3544
mercury-venus	+6.4897	+2.1553	4.3389
mercury-jupiter	+6.9065	+0.6199	6.2878
mercury-I-plane	+6.8380	+0.4948	6.3453
mercury-pluto	+0.4958	15.6043	15.225
mercury-saturn	+6.5420	+0.1585	6.3896
mercury-neptune	+6.7755	-0.2485	7.0273
mars-uranus	+1.7812	+0.5884	1.1929
mars-Sun	+1.5395	+7.1762	5.6376
mars-venus	+1.1218	+3.0574	1.9363
mars-jupiter	+1.3136	-0.1231	1.4371
mars-I-plane	+1.1113	-0.5636	1.6755
mars-pluto	+0.7405	17.0807	16.348
mars-saturn	-0.5920	+1.7714	2.3645
mars-neptune	+1.2434	-1.1350	2.3790
uranus-Sun	+0.7726	+7.2500	6.4774
uranus-venus	+0.7717	+3.3934	2.6217
uranus-jupiter	+0.4455	+1.1463	0.7008
uranus-I-plane	+0.4168	+1.4431	1.0264
uranus-pluto	+0.6112	17.1629	16.552
uranus-saturn	+0.4670	+2.4133	1.9567
uranus-neptune	+0.0982	+1.6056	1.5075
Sun-venus	+7.2483	+3.3900	3.8533
Sun-jupiter	+7.2196	+1.1302	6.0898
Sun-I-plane	+7.1766	+1.2072	5.9703

Interface: Planetary Nodes

	SQ1:LAT	SQ2:LAT	ANGLE
Sun-pluto	+4.1248	16.0451	11.987
Sun-saturn	+6.9563	+1.4421	5.5177
Sun-neptune	+7.0537	-+0.6217	6.4348
venus-jupiter	+3.3003	+1.0437	2.2568
venus-I-plane	+3.1521	+0.9633	2.1893
venus-pluto	+2.5524	17.0418	14.474
venus-saturn	+2.3168	+0.2653	2.0534
venus-neptune	+2.8910	+0.1110	2.7814
jupiter-I-plane	+1.0463	+1.3740	0.3278
jupiter-pluto	+1.2844	17.1679	15.884
jupiter-saturn	+1.1634	+2.4194	1.2561
jupiter-neptune	+0.2939	+1.2405	0.9469
I-plane-pluto	+1.5803	17.1696	15.589
I-plane-saturn	+1.5160	+2.4505	0.9346
I-plane-neptune	+0.0898	+0.8169	0.7275
pluto-saturn	17.1691	+2.4876	14.682
pluto-neptune	17.1546	+1.6343	15.521
saturn-neptune	+2.0572	+1.0892	0.9684

Interface: Planetary Nodes

Reading the Interface Tables

In the following pages, there are Interface Tables for 1900, 1950, and 2000. The all follow the same format, so let's go over it.

```
01°Ar02'  MA-NE  01°Li02'
04°Ar02'  MA-JU  04°Li02'
09°Ar27'  EA*JU  09°Li27'
11°Ar31'  VE+MA  11°Li31'
```

The first listing is "01°Ar02'," which is for the Mars-Neptune interface. It's opposite nodal point is "01°Li02'." Two planetary names linked by a hyphen indicate the zodiac position of that node for the particular epoch. The next listing is for the interface node for Mars-Jupiter.

The third listing "11°Ar31'" is for Square Point for Venus-Mars, and this is indicated by the "+" which stands here for "Square Point." It's opposite Square Point is at "11°Li31'" which is in zodiac terms 11 degrees of Libra 31'.

MA-NE
A dash between two planets: an Interface Point.

EA*JU
An "*" between two planets: Interface Point to Earth.

VE+MA
A "+" between two planets: Square Point.

Interface Points epoch 1900.0

```
01°Ar02'  MA-NE  01°Li02'
04°Ar02'  MA-JU  04°Li02'
09°Ar27'  EA*JU  09°Li27'
11°Ar31'  VE+MA  11°Li31'
13°Ar20'  IP-NE  13°Li20'
16°Ar35'  NE+PL  16°Li35'
16°Ar35'  EA*IP  16°Li35'
18°Ar19'  SA+PL  18°Li19'
18°Ar57'  EA*PL  18°Li57'
19°Ar13'  PL+IP  19°Li13'
19°Ar47'  PL+JU  19°Li47'
20°Ar36'  PL+UR  20°Li36'
22°Ar47'  EA*SA  22°Li47'
24°Ar57'  PL+MA  24°Li57'
25°Ar16'  ME-VE  25°Li16'
26°Ar26'  ME-SA  26°Li26'
26°Ar46'  PL+VE  26°Li46'
28°Ar54'  VE-SA  28°Li54'
02°Ta39'  ME-NE  02°Sc39'
03°Ta06'  MA-UR  03°Sc06'
03°Ta21'  SA+IP  03°Sc21'
04°Ta48'  ME-IP  04°Sc48'
06°Ta43'  SA+JU  06°Sc43'
07°Ta17'  SA+UR  07°Sc17'
07°Ta43'  ME-JU  07°Sc43'
08°Ta17'  JU+UR  08°Sc17'
10°Ta10'  PL+SU  10°Sc10'
10°Ta41'  EA*NE  10°Sc41'
10°Ta51'  IP+UR  10°Sc51'
14°Ta03'  ME-UR  14°Sc03'
14°Ta15'  VE-NE  14°Sc15'
14°Ta17'  PL+ME  14°Sc17'
16°Ta21'  IP+JU  16°Sc21'
16°Ta34'  ME-MA  16°Sc34'
17°Ta09'  ME+NE  17°Sc09'
17°Ta09'  ME+SA  17°Sc09'
17°Ta09'  ME+PL  17°Sc09'
17°Ta09'  ME+IP  17°Sc09'
17°Ta09'  ME+JU  17°Sc09'
17°Ta09'  ME+VE  17°Sc09'
17°Ta09'  ME+SU  17°Sc09'
17°Ta09'  ME+UR  17°Sc09'
17°Ta09'  ME+MA  17°Sc09'
17°Ta09'  EA-ME  17°Sc09'
18°Ta47'  MA+NE  18°Sc47'
18°Ta47'  MA+SA  18°Sc47'
18°Ta47'  MA+PL  18°Sc47'
18°Ta47'  MA+IP  18°Sc47'
18°Ta47'  MA+JU  18°Sc47'
18°Ta47'  MA+VE  18°Sc47'
18°Ta47'  MA+SU  18°Sc47'
18°Ta47'  MA+UR  18°Sc47'
18°Ta47'  EA-MA  18°Sc47'
```

Interface: Planetary Nodes

```
24°Ta05'  VE-IP  24°Sc05'
26°Ta53'  SU+ME  26°Sc53'
28°Ta10'  SU-SA  28°Sc10'
01°Ge09'  SU-NE  01°Sa09'
02°Ge20'  VE-JU  02°Sa20'
06°Ge12'  NE+UR  06°Sa12'
06°Ge17'  SU-IP  06°Sa17'
07°Ge31'  SA+MA  07°Sa31'
09°Ge10'  SU-JU  09°Sa10'
13°Ge08'  SU-VE  13°Sa08'
13°Ge29'  UR+NE  13°Sa29'
13°Ge29'  UR+SA  13°Sa29'
13°Ge29'  UR+PL  13°Sa29'
13°Ge29'  UR+IP  13°Sa29'
13°Ge29'  UR+JU  13°Sa29'
13°Ge29'  UR+VE  13°Sa29'
13°Ge29'  UR+SU  13°Sa29'
13°Ge29'  EA-UR  13°Sa29'
14°Ge22'  SU+NE  14°Sa22'
14°Ge22'  SU+SA  14°Sa22'
14°Ge22'  SU+PL  14°Sa22'
14°Ge22'  SU+IP  14°Sa22'
14°Ge22'  SU+JU  14°Sa22'
14°Ge22'  SU+VE  14°Sa22'
14°Ge22'  EA-SU  14°Sa22'
14°Ge28'  UR-SU  14°Sa28'
15°Ge47'  VE+NE  15°Sa47'
15°Ge47'  VE+SA  15°Sa47'
15°Ge47'  VE+PL  15°Sa47'
15°Ge47'  VE+IP  15°Sa47'
15°Ge47'  VE+JU  15°Sa47'
15°Ge47'  EA-VE  15°Sa47'
16°Ge27'  UR-VE  16°Sa27'
18°Ge27'  SA-NE  18°Sa27'
22°Ge28'  MA-SU  22°Sa28'
25°Ge44'  IP+MA  25°Sa44'
26°Ge29'  NE+JU  26°Sa29'
01°Cn03'  NE+MA  01°Cp03'
04°Cn02'  JU+MA  04°Cp02'
09°Cn27'  JU+NE  09°Cp27'
09°Cn27'  JU+SA  09°Cp27'
09°Cn27'  JU+PL  09°Cp27'
09°Cn27'  JU+IP  09°Cp27'
09°Cn27'  EA-JU  09°Cp27'
11°Cn27'  MA-VE  11°Cp27'
13°Cn21'  NE+IP  13°Cp21'
16°Cn35'  IP+NE  16°Cp35'
16°Cn35'  IP+SA  16°Cp35'
16°Cn35'  IP+PL  16°Cp35'
16°Cn35'  EA-IP  16°Cp35'
16°Cn36'  PL-NE  16°Cp36'
18°Cn20'  PL-SA  18°Cp20'
18°Cn57'  PL+NE  18°Cp57'
18°Cn57'  PL+SA  18°Cp57'
18°Cn57'  EA-PL  18°Cp57'
```

Interface: Planetary Nodes

```
19°Cn11'  IP-PL  19°Cp11'
19°Cn43'  JU-PL  19°Cp43'
20°Cn28'  UR-PL  20°Cp28'
22°Cn47'  SA+NE  22°Cp47'
22°Cn47'  EA-SA  22°Cp47'
24°Cn26'  MA-PL  24°Cp26'
25°Cn11'  VE+ME  25°Cp11'
26°Cn06'  VE-PL  26°Cp06'
26°Cn26'  SA+ME  26°Cp26'
28°Cn53'  SA+VE  28°Cp53'
02°Le39'  NE+ME  02°Aq39'
03°Le06'  UR+MA  03°Aq06'
03°Le20'  IP-SA  03°Aq20'
04°Le48'  IP+ME  04°Aq48'
06°Le42'  JU-SA  06°Aq42'
07°Le16'  UR-SA  07°Aq16'
07°Le42'  JU+ME  07°Aq42'
08°Le17'  UR-JU  08°Aq17'
08°Le28'  SU-PL  08°Aq28'
10°Le41'  EA-NE  10°Aq41'
10°Le50'  UR-IP  10°Aq50'
12°Le20'  ME-PL  12°Aq20'
14°Le03'  UR+ME  14°Aq03'
14°Le15'  NE+VE  14°Aq15'
16°Le20'  JU-IP  16°Aq20'
16°Le34'  MA+ME  16°Aq34'
17°Le09'  EA*ME  17°Aq09'
18°Le47'  EA*MA  18°Aq47'
24°Le03'  IP+VE  24°Aq03'
26°Le37'  ME-SU  26°Aq37'
28°Le07'  SA+SU  28°Aq07'
01°Vi07'  NE+SU  01°Pi07'
02°Vi20'  JU+VE  02°Pi20'
06°Vi11'  UR-NE  06°Pi11'
06°Vi16'  IP+SU  06°Pi16'
07°Vi28'  MA-SA  07°Pi28'
09°Vi10'  JU+SU  09°Pi10'
13°Vi07'  VE+SU  13°Pi07'
13°Vi29'  EA*UR  13°Pi29'
14°Vi22'  EA*SU  14°Pi22'
14°Vi28'  SU+UR  14°Pi28'
15°Vi47'  EA*VE  15°Pi47'
16°Vi28'  VE+UR  16°Pi28'
18°Vi25'  NE+SA  18°Pi25'
22°Vi35'  SU+MA  22°Pi35'
25°Vi43'  MA-IP  25°Pi43'
26°Vi28'  JU-NE  26°Pi28'
```

Interface Points epoch 1950.0

```
01°Ar02'  MA-NE  01°Li02'
04°Ar02'  MA-JU  04°Li02'
09°Ar27'  EA*JU  09°Li27'
11°Ar31'  VE+MA  11°Li31'
13°Ar20'  IP-NE  13°Li20'
16°Ar35'  NE+PL  16°Li35'
16°Ar35'  EA*IP  16°Li35'
18°Ar19'  SA+PL  18°Li19'
18°Ar57'  EA*PL  18°Li57'
19°Ar13'  PL+IP  19°Li13'
19°Ar47'  PL+JU  19°Li47'
20°Ar36'  PL+UR  20°Li36'
22°Ar47'  EA*SA  22°Li47'
24°Ar57'  PL+MA  24°Li57'
25°Ar16'  ME-VE  25°Li16'
26°Ar26'  ME-SA  26°Li26'
26°Ar46'  PL+VE  26°Li46'
28°Ar54'  VE-SA  28°Li54'
02°Ta39'  ME-NE  02°Sc39'
03°Ta06'  MA-UR  03°Sc06'
03°Ta21'  SA+IP  03°Sc21'
04°Ta48'  ME-IP  04°Sc48'
06°Ta43'  SA+JU  06°Sc43'
07°Ta17'  SA+UR  07°Sc17'
07°Ta43'  ME-JU  07°Sc43'
08°Ta17'  JU+UR  08°Sc17'
10°Ta10'  PL+SU  10°Sc10'
10°Ta41'  EA*NE  10°Sc41'
10°Ta51'  IP+UR  10°Sc51'
14°Ta03'  ME-UR  14°Sc03'
14°Ta15'  VE-NE  14°Sc15'
14°Ta17'  PL+ME  14°Sc17'
16°Ta21'  IP+JU  16°Sc21'
16°Ta34'  ME-MA  16°Sc34'
17°Ta09'  ME+NE  17°Sc09'
17°Ta09'  ME+SA  17°Sc09'
17°Ta09'  ME+PL  17°Sc09'
17°Ta09'  ME+IP  17°Sc09'
17°Ta09'  ME+JU  17°Sc09'
17°Ta09'  ME+VE  17°Sc09'
17°Ta09'  ME+SU  17°Sc09'
17°Ta09'  ME+UR  17°Sc09'
17°Ta09'  ME+MA  17°Sc09'
17°Ta09'  EA-ME  17°Sc09'
18°Ta47'  MA+NE  18°Sc47'
18°Ta47'  MA+SA  18°Sc47'
18°Ta47'  MA+PL  18°Sc47'
18°Ta47'  MA+IP  18°Sc47'
18°Ta47'  MA+JU  18°Sc47'
18°Ta47'  MA+VE  18°Sc47'
18°Ta47'  MA+SU  18°Sc47'
```

Interface: Planetary Nodes

```
18°Ta47'  MA+UR  18°Sc47'
18°Ta47'  EA-MA  18°Sc47'
24°Ta05'  VE-IP  24°Sc05'
26°Ta53'  SU+ME  26°Sc53'
28°Ta10'  SU-SA  28°Sc10'
01°Ge09'  SU-NE  01°Sa09'
02°Ge20'  VE-JU  02°Sa20'
06°Ge12'  NE+UR  06°Sa12'
06°Ge17'  SU-IP  06°Sa17'
07°Ge31'  SA+MA  07°Sa31'
09°Ge10'  SU-JU  09°Sa10'
13°Ge08'  SU-VE  13°Sa08'
13°Ge29'  UR+NE  13°Sa29'
13°Ge29'  UR+SA  13°Sa29'
13°Ge29'  UR+PL  13°Sa29'
13°Ge29'  UR+IP  13°Sa29'
13°Ge29'  UR+JU  13°Sa29'
13°Ge29'  UR+VE  13°Sa29'
13°Ge29'  UR+SU  13°Sa29'
13°Ge29'  EA-UR  13°Sa29'
14°Ge22'  SU+NE  14°Sa22'
14°Ge22'  SU+SA  14°Sa22'
14°Ge22'  SU+PL  14°Sa22'
14°Ge22'  SU+IP  14°Sa22'
14°Ge22'  SU+JU  14°Sa22'
14°Ge22'  SU+VE  14°Sa22'
14°Ge22'  EA-SU  14°Sa22'
14°Ge28'  UR-SU  14°Sa28'
15°Ge47'  VE+NE  15°Sa47'
15°Ge47'  VE+SA  15°Sa47'
15°Ge47'  VE+PL  15°Sa47'
15°Ge47'  VE+IP  15°Sa47'
15°Ge47'  VE+JU  15°Sa47'
15°Ge47'  EA-VE  15°Sa47'
16°Ge27'  UR-VE  16°Sa27'
18°Ge27'  SA-NE  18°Sa27'
22°Ge28'  MA-SU  22°Sa28'
25°Ge44'  IP+MA  25°Sa44'
26°Ge29'  NE+JU  26°Sa29'
01°Cn03'  NE+MA  01°Cp03'
04°Cn02'  JU+MA  04°Cp02'
09°Cn27'  JU+NE  09°Cp27'
09°Cn27'  JU+SA  09°Cp27'
09°Cn27'  JU+PL  09°Cp27'
09°Cn27'  JU+IP  09°Cp27'
09°Cn27'  EA-JU  09°Cp27'
11°Cn27'  MA-VE  11°Cp27'
13°Cn21'  NE+IP  13°Cp21'
16°Cn35'  IP+NE  16°Cp35'
16°Cn35'  IP+SA  16°Cp35'
16°Cn35'  IP+PL  16°Cp35'
16°Cn35'  EA-IP  16°Cp35'
16°Cn36'  PL-NE  16°Cp36'
18°Cn20'  PL-SA  18°Cp20'
18°Cn57'  PL+NE  18°Cp57'
```

Interface: Planetary Nodes

```
18°Cn57'  PL+SA  18°Cp57'
18°Cn57'  EA-PL  18°Cp57'
19°Cn11'  IP-PL  19°Cp11'
19°Cn43'  JU-PL  19°Cp43'
20°Cn28'  UR-PL  20°Cp28'
22°Cn47'  SA+NE  22°Cp47'
22°Cn47'  EA-SA  22°Cp47'
24°Cn26'  MA-PL  24°Cp26'
25°Cn11'  VE+ME  25°Cp11'
26°Cn06'  VE-PL  26°Cp06'
26°Cn26'  SA+ME  26°Cp26'
28°Cn53'  SA+VE  28°Cp53'
02°Le39'  NE+ME  02°Aq39'
03°Le06'  UR+MA  03°Aq06'
03°Le20'  IP-SA  03°Aq20'
04°Le48'  IP+ME  04°Aq48'
06°Le42'  JU-SA  06°Aq42'
07°Le16'  UR-SA  07°Aq16'
07°Le42'  JU+ME  07°Aq42'
08°Le17'  UR-JU  08°Aq17'
08°Le28'  SU-PL  08°Aq28'
10°Le41'  EA-NE  10°Aq41'
10°Le50'  UR-IP  10°Aq50'
12°Le20'  ME-PL  12°Aq20'
14°Le03'  UR+ME  14°Aq03'
14°Le15'  NE+VE  14°Aq15'
16°Le20'  JU-IP  16°Aq20'
16°Le34'  MA+ME  16°Aq34'
17°Le09'  EA*ME  17°Aq09'
18°Le47'  EA*MA  18°Aq47'
24°Le03'  IP+VE  24°Aq03'
26°Le37'  ME-SU  26°Aq37'
28°Le07'  SA+SU  28°Aq07'
01°Vi07'  NE+SU  01°Pi07'
02°Vi20'  JU+VE  02°Pi20'
06°Vi11'  UR-NE  06°Pi11'
06°Vi16'  IP+SU  06°Pi16'
07°Vi28'  MA-SA  07°Pi28'
09°Vi10'  JU+SU  09°Pi10'
13°Vi07'  VE+SU  13°Pi07'
13°Vi29'  EA*UR  13°Pi29'
14°Vi22'  EA*SU  14°Pi22'
14°Vi28'  SU+UR  14°Pi28'
15°Vi47'  EA*VE  15°Pi47'
16°Vi28'  VE+UR  16°Pi28'
18°Vi25'  NE+SA  18°Pi25'
22°Vi35'  SU+MA  22°Pi35'
25°Vi43'  MA-IP  25°Pi43'
26°Vi28'  JU-NE  26°Pi28'
```

Interface Points, epoch 2000.0

```
02°Ar07'  MA-NE  02°Li07'
05°Ar02'  MA-JU  05°Li02'
10°Ar27'  EA*JU  10°Li27'
12°Ar28'  VE+MA  12°Li28'
15°Ar31'  IP-NE  15°Li31'
17°Ar33'  EA*IP  17°Li33'
18°Ar01'  NE+PL  18°Li01'
19°Ar48'  SA+PL  19°Li48'
20°Ar21'  EA*PL  20°Li21'
20°Ar39'  PL+IP  20°Li39'
21°Ar12'  PL+JU  21°Li12'
22°Ar02'  PL+UR  22°Li02'
23°Ar40'  EA*SA  23°Li40'
26°Ar22'  PL+MA  26°Li22'
26°Ar36'  ME-VE  26°Li36'
27°Ar40'  ME-SA  27°Li40'
28°Ar16'  PL+VE  28°Li16'
29°Ar56'  VE-SA  29°Li56'
03°Ta54'  ME-NE  03°Sc54'
03°Ta59'  MA-UR  03°Sc59'
04°Ta13'  SA+IP  04°Sc13'
05°Ta58'  ME-IP  05°Sc58'
07°Ta23'  SA+JU  07°Sc23'
08°Ta18'  SA+UR  08°Sc18'
08°Ta58'  ME-JU  08°Sc58'
09°Ta53'  JU+UR  09°Sc53'
11°Ta34'  PL+SU  11°Sc34'
11°Ta47'  EA*NE  11°Sc47'
11°Ta55'  IP+UR  11°Sc55'
15°Ta19'  ME-UR  15°Sc19'
15°Ta21'  VE-NE  15°Sc21'
15°Ta42'  PL+ME  15°Sc42'
16°Ta09'  IP+JU  16°Sc09'
17°Ta54'  ME-MA  17°Sc54'
18°Ta20'  ME+NE  18°Sc20'
18°Ta20'  ME+SA  18°Sc20'
18°Ta20'  ME+PL  18°Sc20'
18°Ta20'  ME+IP  18°Sc20'
18°Ta20'  ME+JU  18°Sc20'
18°Ta20'  ME+VE  18°Sc20'
18°Ta20'  ME+SU  18°Sc20'
18°Ta20'  ME+UR  18°Sc20'
18°Ta20'  ME+MA  18°Sc20'
18°Ta20'  EA-ME  18°Sc20'
19°Ta33'  MA+NE  19°Sc33'
19°Ta33'  MA+SA  19°Sc33'
19°Ta33'  MA+PL  19°Sc33'
19°Ta33'  MA+IP  19°Sc33'
19°Ta33'  MA+JU  19°Sc33'
19°Ta33'  MA+VE  19°Sc33'
19°Ta33'  MA+SU  19°Sc33'
19°Ta33'  MA+UR  19°Sc33'
```

272

Interface: Planetary Nodes

```
19°Ta33'  EA-MA  19°Sc33'
24°Ta52'  VE-IP  24°Sc52'
28°Ta14'  SU+ME  28°Sc14'
29°Ta44'  SU-SA  29°Sc44'
02°Ge39'  SU-NE  02°Sa39'
03°Ge17'  VE-JU  03°Sa17'
07°Ge31'  NE+UR  07°Sa31'
07°Ge45'  SU-IP  07°Sa45'
08°Ge25'  SA+MA  08°Sa25'
10°Ge40'  SU-JU  10°Sa40'
13°Ge59'  UR+NE  13°Sa59'
13°Ge59'  UR+SA  13°Sa59'
13°Ge59'  UR+PL  13°Sa59'
13°Ge59'  UR+IP  13°Sa59'
13°Ge59'  UR+JU  13°Sa59'
13°Ge59'  UR+VE  13°Sa59'
13°Ge59'  UR+SU  13°Sa59'
13°Ge59'  EA-UR  13°Sa59'
14°Ge58'  SU-VE  14°Sa58'
15°Ge46'  SU+NE  15°Sa46'
15°Ge46'  SU+SA  15°Sa46'
15°Ge46'  SU+PL  15°Sa46'
15°Ge46'  SU+IP  15°Sa46'
15°Ge46'  SU+JU  15°Sa46'
15°Ge46'  SU+VE  15°Sa46'
15°Ge46'  EA-SU  15°Sa46'
15°Ge59'  UR-SU  15°Sa59'
16°Ge41'  VE+NE  16°Sa41'
16°Ge41'  VE+SA  16°Sa41'
16°Ge41'  VE+PL  16°Sa41'
16°Ge41'  VE+IP  16°Sa41'
16°Ge41'  VE+JU  16°Sa41'
16°Ge41'  EA-VE  16°Sa41'
17°Ge29'  UR-VE  17°Sa29'
19°Ge23'  SA-NE  19°Sa23'
24°Ge02'  MA-SU  24°Sa02'
26°Ge23'  IP+MA  26°Sa23'
27°Ge42'  NE+JU  27°Sa42'
02°Cn09'  NE+MA  02°Cp09'
05°Cn02'  JU+MA  05°Cp02'
10°Cn27'  JU+NE  10°Cp27'
10°Cn27'  JU+SA  10°Cp27'
10°Cn27'  JU+PL  10°Cp27'
10°Cn27'  JU+IP  10°Cp27'
10°Cn27'  EA-JU  10°Cp27'
12°Cn24'  MA-VE  12°Cp24'
15°Cn32'  NE+IP  15°Cp32'
17°Cn33'  IP+NE  17°Cp33'
17°Cn33'  IP+SA  17°Cp33'
17°Cn33'  IP+PL  17°Cp33'
17°Cn33'  EA-IP  17°Cp33'
18°Cn02'  PL-NE  18°Cp02'
19°Cn48'  PL-SA  19°Cp48'
20°Cn21'  PL+NE  20°Cp21'
20°Cn21'  PL+SA  20°Cp21'
```

273

Interface: Planetary Nodes

```
20°Cn21'  EA-PL  20°Cp21'
20°Cn38'  IP-PL  20°Cp38'
21°Cn08'  JU-PL  21°Cp08'
21°Cn53'  UR-PL  21°Cp53'
23°Cn40'  SA+NE  23°Cp40'
23°Cn40'  EA-SA  23°Cp40'
25°Cn51'  MA-PL  25°Cp51'
26°Cn30'  VE+ME  26°Cp30'
27°Cn35'  VE-PL  27°Cp35'
27°Cn40'  SA+ME  27°Cp40'
29°Cn55'  SA+VE  29°Cp55'
03°Le55'  NE+ME  03°Aq55'
03°Le58'  UR+MA  03°Aq58'
04°Le12'  IP-SA  04°Aq12'
05°Le57'  IP+ME  05°Aq57'
07°Le22'  JU-SA  07°Aq22'
08°Le16'  UR-SA  08°Aq16'
08°Le57'  JU+ME  08°Aq57'
09°Le52'  SU-PL  09°Aq52'
09°Le53'  UR-JU  09°Aq53'
11°Le47'  EA-NE  11°Aq47'
11°Le54'  UR-IP  11°Aq54'
13°Le44'  ME-PL  13°Aq44'
15°Le18'  UR+ME  15°Aq18'
15°Le21'  NE+VE  15°Aq21'
16°Le08'  JU-IP  16°Aq08'
17°Le54'  MA+ME  17°Aq54'
18°Le20'  EA*ME  18°Aq20'
19°Le33'  EA*MA  19°Aq33'
24°Le50'  IP+VE  24°Aq50'
27°Le59'  ME-SU  27°Aq59'
29°Le41'  SA+SU  29°Aq41'
02°Vi38'  NE+SU  02°Pi38'
03°Vi16'  JU+VE  03°Pi16'
07°Vi30'  UR-NE  07°Pi30'
07°Vi44'  IP+SU  07°Pi44'
08°Vi22'  MA-SA  08°Pi22'
10°Vi40'  JU+SU  10°Pi40'
13°Vi59'  EA*UR  13°Pi59'
14°Vi58'  VE+SU  14°Pi58'
15°Vi46'  EA*SU  15°Pi46'
15°Vi59'  SU+UR  15°Pi59'
16°Vi41'  EA*VE  16°Pi41'
17°Vi29'  VE+UR  17°Pi29'
19°Vi22'  NE+SA  19°Pi22'
24°Vi10'  SU+MA  24°Pi10'
26°Vi22'  MA-IP  26°Pi22'
27°Vi40'  JU-NE  27°Pi40'
```

Michael Erlewine

Internationally known astrologer and author Noel Tyl (author of 34 books on astrology) has this to say about Michael Erlewine:

Michael Erlewine

"Michael Erlewine is the giant influence whose creativity is forever imprinted on all astrologers' work

all astrologers' work since the beginning of the Computer era! He is the man who single-handedly applied computer technology to astrological measurement, research, and interpretation, and has been the formative and leading light of astrology's modern growth. Erlewine humanized it all, adding perception and incisive practical analyses to modern, computerized astrology. Now, for a second generation of astrologers and their public, Erlewine's genius continues with StarTypes ... and it's simply amazing!"

Interface: Planetary Nodes

A Brief Bio of Michael Erlewine

Michael Erlewine has studied and practiced astrology for over 40 years, as an author, teacher, lecturer, personal consultant, programmer, and conference producer.

Erlewine was the first astrologer to program astrology, on microcomputers and make those programs available to his fellow astrologers. This was in 1977. He founded Matrix Astrology in 1978, and his company, along with Microsoft, are the two oldest software companies still on the Internet.

Michael, soon joined by his astrologer-brother Stephen Erlewine, went on to revolutionize astrology by producing, for the new microcomputers, the first written astrological reports, first research system, first high resolution chart wheels, geographic and star maps, and on and on.

Along the way Matrix produced programs that spoke astrology (audio), personal astrological videos, infomercials, and many other pioneering feats.

Michael Erlewine has received major awards from UAC (United Astrological Conferences), AFA (American Federation of Astrologers), and the PIA (Professional Astrologers Incorporated), and scores of online awards.

Michael and Stephen Erlewine have published a yearly calendar for almost 30 years, since 1969. Michael Erlewine has produced and put on more than 36 conferences in the areas of astrology and Buddhism.

Example Astro*Image Card

Aside from his current work as a consultant for NBC's iVillage and Astrology.com, Erlewine has personally designed over 6,000 tarot-like astrology cards, making authentic astrology available to people with little or no experience in the topic. These Astro*Image™ cards are available through a variety of small astrological programs and in eBooks. Some examples can be found at WWW.StarTypes.com, where there is also a link to his astrological software.

Personal Astrology Readings

Michael Erlewine has been doing personal astrology readings for almost forty years and enjoys sharing his knowledge with others. However, his busy schedule makes it difficult to honor all requests. However, feel free to email (Michael@Erlewine.net) him if you wish a personal chart reading. He will let you know if his current schedule will allow him to work with you.

The sections that follow will give you more details about Michael Erlewine and his very active center.

The Heart Center House

In 1972, Michael and Margaret Erlewine established the Heart Center, a center for community studies. Today, the Heart Center continues to be a center for astrological and spiritual work. Over the years, hundreds of invited guests have stayed at the Heart Center, some for just a night, others for many years. Astrologers, authors, musicians, Sanskrit scholars, swamis - you name it, the Heart Center has been a home for a wide group of individuals, all united by their interest in spiritual or cultural ideas.

Heart Center Library

Erlewine also founded and directs The Heart Center Astrological Library, the largest astrological library in the United States, and probably the world, that is open to researchers. Meticulously catalogued, the current library project is the scanning of the Table of Contents for all major books and periodicals on astrology.

The library does not have regular hours, so contact ahead of time if you wish to visit. Michael@erlewine.net.

The All-Music Guide / All-Movie Guide

Michael Erlewine's devotion to studying and playing the music of Black Americans, in particular blues, led to his traveling to small blues clubs of Chicago and hearing live, blues greats like Little Walter, Magic Sam, Big Walter Horton, and many others. He went on to interview many dozens of performers. Much of this interviewing took place at the Ann Arbor Blues Festivals, in 1969 and 1970, the first electric blues festivals of any size ever held in North America, and than later at the Ann Arbor Blues & Jazz Festivals.

With their extensive knowledge of the blues music, Erlewine and his brother Daniel were asked to play host to the score or so of professional blues musicians and their bands. They were in charge of serving them food and (of course) drink. Michael went on to interview most of the performers in these early festivals, with an audio recorder, and later on with video.

The interviewing led to more study and ultimately resulted in Michael founding and developing AMG, the All-Music Guide, today the largest single database of music reviews and documentation on the planet.

Erlewine started from a one-room office, and the reviewers and music aficionados of the time laughed at his attempt to cover all music. But he persisted, and the all-Music Guide appeared as a Gopher Site, before the World Wide Web even existed-a database of popular music for all music lovers.

Over the years AMG grew, and the All-Movie Guide and All Game Guide were born, and also flourished. Later, Erlewine would create ClassicPosters.com, devoted to the history and documentation of rock n' roll posters, some 35,000 of them.

These guides changed the way music was reviewed and rated. Previous to AMG, review guides like the "Rolling Stones Record Guide" were run by a few sophisticated reviewers, and the emphasis was on the expertise of the reviewer, and their point of view. Erlewine insisted on treating all artists equally, and not comparing artist to artist, what can be important, Michael points out, is to find the best music any artist has produced, not if the artist is better or worse than Jimmie Hendrix or Bob Dylan.

Erlewine sold AMG in 1996, at which time he had 150 fulltime employees, and 500 free-lance writers. He had edited and published any number of books and CD-ROMs on music and film. During the time he owned and ran AMG, there were no advertisements on the site and nothing for sale. As Erlewine writes, "All of us deserve to have access to our own popular culture. That is what AMG and ClassicPosters.com are all about." Today, AMG reviews can be found everywhere across the Internet. Erlewine's music collection is housed in an AMG warehouse, numbering almost 500,000 CDs.

Heart Center Meditation Room

Michael Erlewine has been active in Buddhism since the 1950s. Here are his own words:

"Back in the late 1950s, and early 1960, Buddhism was one of many ideas we stayed up late, smoked cigarettes, drank lots of coffee, and talked about, along with existentialism, poetry, and the like.

"It was not until I met the Tibetan lama, Chogyam Trungpa Rinpoche, in 1974 that I understood Buddhism as not just Philosophy, but also as path, a way to get through life. Having been raised Catholic, serving as an altar boy, learning church Latin, and all that, I had not been given any kind of a path, other than the path of faith. I hung onto that faith as long as I could, but it told me very little about how to live and work in this world.,

"I had been trying to learn the basics of Tibetan Buddhism before I met Trungpa Rinpoche, but the spark that welded all of that together was missing. Trungpa provided that spark. I got to be his chauffer for a weekend, and to design a poster for his public talk.

"More important, only about an hour after we met, Trungpa took me into a small room for a couple of hours and taught me to meditate. I didn't even understand what I was learning. All that I know was that I was learning about myself.

"After that meeting, I begin to understand a lot more of what I had read, but it was almost ten years later that I met my teacher, Khenpo Karthar, Rinpoche, the abbot of Karma Triyana Dharmachakra Monstery, in the mountains above Woodstock, NY. Meeting Rinpoche was life-changing.

Heart Center Symbol

"It was not long after that we started the Heart Center Meditation Center here in Big Rapids, which is still going today. My wife and I became more and more involved with the monastery in New York, and we ended up serving on several boards, and even as fundraisers for the monastery. We helped to raise the funds to build a 3-year retreat in upstate New York, one for men and one for women.

"We also established KTD Dharma Goods, a mail-order dharma goods business that helped practitioners find the meditation materials they might need. We published many sadhanas, the traditional Buddhist practice texts, plus other teachings, in print and on audio tape.

Years have gone by, and I am still working with Khenpo, Rinpoche and the sangha at the Woodstock monastery. Some years ago, Rinpoche surprised my wife and I by telling us we should go to Tibet and meet His Holiness the 17th Karmapa, and that we should go right away, that summer, and I hate to leave the house!

That trip, and a second trip that followed some years later, turned out to be pilgrimages that were also life changing. Our center in Big Rapids has a separate building as a shrine room and even a small Stupa; pictures are shown below.

I can never repay the kindness that Khenpo Rinpoche and the other rinpoches that I have taken teachings from have shown me.

Music Career

Michael Erlewine's career in music started early on, when he dropped out of high school and hitchhiked to Venice West, in Santa Monica, California, in an attempt to catch a ride on the tail end of the Beatnik era. This was 1960, and he was a little late for that, but right on time for the folk music revival that was just beginning to bloom at that time. Like many other people his age, Erlewine traveled from college center to center across the nation: Ann Arbor, Berkeley, Cambridge, and Greenwich Village. There was a well-beaten track on which traveled the young folk musicians of the future.

Erlewine, who also played folk guitar, hitchhiked for a stint with a young Bob Dylan, and then more extensively with guitar virtuoso and instrumentalist Perry Lederman. Erlewine helped to put on Dylan's first concert in Ann Arbor. He hung out with people like Ramblin' Jack Elliot, Joan Baez, The New Lost City Ramblers, and the County Gentlemen.

Interface: Planetary Nodes

In 1965, the same year that the Grateful Dead were forming, Michael Erlewine, his brother Daniel, and a few others formed the first new-style band in the Midwest, the Prime Movers Blues Band. Iggy Pop was their drummer, and his stint in the band was how he got the name Iggy. This was the beginning of the hippie era. Michael was the band's lead singer, and played amplified Chicago-style blues harmonica. He still plays.

Erlewine was also the manager of the band, and personally designed and silkscreened the band's posters, one of which is shown below.

The Prime Movers became a seminal band throughout the Midwest, and even traveled as far as the West Coast, where the band spent 1967, the "summer of Love," playing at all of the famous clubs, for example, opening for Eric Clapton and Cream, at the Fillmore Auditorium.

As the 60s wound down, and bands began to break up, Erlewine was still studying the music of American Blacks, in particular blues. Because of their knowledge of blues and the players, Michael and his brother Dan were invited to help host the first major electric blues festival in the United States, the 1969 Ann Arbor Blues Festival. They got to wine and dine the performers, and generally look after them.

Michael interviewed (audio and video) most of the players at the first two Ann Arbor Blues Festivals, they included: Big Joe Turner, Luther Allison, Carey Bell, Bobby Bland, Clifton Chenier, James Cotton, Pee Wee Crayton, Arthur, Crudup, Jimmy Dawkins, Doctor Ross, Sleepy John Estes, Lowell Fulson, Buddy Guy, John Lee hooker, Howlin' wolf, J.B. Hutto, Albert King, B.B King, Freddie king, Sam Lay, Light-nin' Hopkins,

Interface: Planetary Nodes

Manse Lipscomb, Robert Lockwood, Magic Sam, Fred Mcdowell, Muddy Waters, Charlie Musslewhite, Louis Myers , Junior Parker, Brewer Phillips, Otis rush, Johnnie Shines, George Smith, Son House, Victoria Spivey, Hubert Sumlin, Sunnyland Slim, Roosevelt Sykes, Eddie Taylor, Hound Dog Taylor, Big mama Thornton, Eddie Vinson, Sippie Wallace, Junior Wells, Big Joe Williams, Robert Pete Williams, Johnny Young, and Mighty Joe Young.

Email:

Michael Erlewine can be reached at Michael@Erlewine.net

Made in the USA
Coppell, TX
08 February 2024

28804918R00160